I0802441

# WASHINGTON, D.C. HOUSING CO-OPS

## A History

Stephen McKevitt

The History PRESS

Published by The History Press
Charleston, SC
www.historypress.com

Copyright © 2021 by DC Cooperative Housing Coalition
All rights reserved

First published 2021

Manufactured in the United States

ISBN 9781467146234

Library of Congress Control Number: 2020945776

*Notice*: The information in this book is true and complete to the best of our knowledge. It is offered without guarantee on the part of the author or The History Press. The author and The History Press disclaim all liability in connection with the use of this book.

All rights reserved. No part of this book may be reproduced or transmitted in any form whatsoever without prior written permission from the publisher except in the case of brief quotations embodied in critical articles and reviews.

# CONTENTS

# FOREWORD

## BY MATTHEW GILMORE

Washington, D.C., has faced challenges in housing its population since its earliest days. President Washington issued regulations encouraging substantial housing, but they were waived for many years. The city grew up with wood-frame dwellings and then moved on to those made of brick. But the scale of housing remained small until the last quarter of the nineteenth century, when larger-scale multifamily buildings were introduced.

The concept of cooperative ownership for multifamily dwellings was introduced to Washington, D.C., in 1920. This was a significant step in the evolution in the District of Columbia's multifamily housing. The genesis began in 1880, when New York congressman Fernando Wood introduced apartment dwelling to the city with his "French flats" at 1418 I Street Northwest. Apartment dwelling quickly became popular, and today, multifamily dwellings house 42 percent of the population of Washington, D.C. As the number of apartment houses ballooned, they grew taller. Regulations followed; limitations on the height of buildings were first introduced in 1899. These height limits, which other cities used to share, gave the city its distinctive skyline.

Regulations on use also followed. On March 1, 1920, legislation was signed to introduce zoning regulations to Washington, D.C. The legislation read, "An act to regulate the height, area, and use of buildings in the District of Columbia and to create a zoning commission and for other purposes." These zoning regulations were no Congressional fiat or imposition. The 1920 Commissioners' Annual Report noted that they had, "for a number of years, been interested in the subject of zoning, which is now universally regarded one of the essential features of a comprehensive city plan." Zoning was modified over time to accommodate the proliferation of apartment houses.

Later in 1920, which also saw the introduction of zoning, real estate developer Allan E. Walker introduced the "Allan E. Walker plan of co-operative ownership." With this plan, owners would invest in shares of a common ownership organization. It was an immediate success. After Walker's early death, Edmund J. Flynn, who was originally part of the Walker firm, promoted and developed a cooperative through his own firm starting in 1922. Today, there are more than one hundred cooperatives in Washington, D.C. In this book, Steve McKevitt tells the story of the century of the city's cooperative housing.

# PREFACE

While the presence—and the history—of cooperative housing goes back to ancient times, 1920 is the year when the modern concept of co-op living sprang forth in Washington, D.C. That year, ten apartment buildings in the city were successfully converted from properties owned by a landlord, who collected rent from the residents, into buildings that were each owned cooperatively by the people who made their homes in the structures. This marked the favorable beginning of the development of the contemporary co-op apartment movement in the nation's capital. The concept was both straightforward and practical. It put the sales of homes in multiunit properties—typically in residential apartment buildings—on essentially the same footing as single-family homes, providing the same benefits to the member-owners that single-family homes offered. It allowed co-op owners to acquire and build up home equity and to benefit from appreciating real estate values. The concept also helped provide affordable housing for a growing middle class.

Not surprisingly, the number of cooperatives grew quickly, and one hundred years after those modest beginnings, there are approximately fifteen thousand cooperative housing units in the District of Columbia. Over the past century, co-ops have helped create and advance the successful growth of many Washington, D.C. neighborhoods. The associations have also provided their residents with the opportunity to live and thrive in urban communities in ways that have facilitated working together with their neighbors for the common good.

The Haddington, a small and attractive cooperative on 1840 Biltmore Street, Northwest, in Adams Morgan. *Photograph by the author.*

Today, thanks to the efforts—past and present—of some very talented and energetic developers, planners and architects, as well as the work of many co-op residents from all walks of life, Washington, D.C., is now home to nearly 150 co-op buildings of various types. Many of these properties are regarded as proud "anchor" buildings in their neighborhoods, and many have been recognized for their architectural distinction. All of them offer the people who live within their walls the opportunity to share in both the responsibilities and the benefits of home ownership with their co-op neighbors.

Of course, this book is not to be taken as a fully inclusive story. The author has tried to cover the major events, the key people and the major cooperatives. A number of smaller co-ops, especially those that are representative of their type or size, have also been reviewed in this book. In the historical narrative of co-op living, the dating by year of larger events can be challenging to pinpoint at times. The dates presented in this book, especially those for construction, are either the years in which buildings opened, the years used by associations today or the years found within the city's many records.

For additional information about the city's various individual co-ops—especially information about these buildings' interiors and special features and their residents—there are a variety of sources that can be consulted. There are numerous books that proudly explore some of Washington, D.C.'s diverse neighborhoods, and each one of these usually covers a particular area's interesting residential history. There are also books that examine the architecture of the city, and there are a few that look at the city's apartment buildings in detail. The District's government and local libraries are also good resources, as each has essential materials. Many co-ops have their own websites, and some have fascinating stories.

In chapter 10, Mike O'Dell of the DC Cooperative Housing Coalition contributes a useful piece that looks at the time ahead. It offers an idea of what the future may hold for Washington, D.C. cooperatives in the next one hundred years.

Since 1984, the DC Cooperative Housing Coalition has served as an advocacy group to champion the interests of cooperatives in the city. The coalition has supported this book to celebrate the one hundredth anniversary of the beginning of housing cooperatives in Washington, D.C. With its many contacts and resources, the coalition's board has assisted in the production of the book and is pleased to help present this tribute. This book covers the history and the multiple benefits of co-op living in the District of Columbia over the past century, and it explores the rich variety of co-op buildings that grace our city.

# ACKNOWLEDGEMENTS

Working on this book has been an interesting experience and one in which I have been able to learn more about our city and its communities and meet some wonderful people. In Washington, D.C., today, it is reassuring to see that so many individuals care about their homes, their neighbors and their city.

I owe a special thanks to Mike O'Dell, the director of the DC Cooperative Housing Coalition, who was the key person who worked with me on developing the details of this book and who then actively helped it along to its completion. I would also like to thank Russ Rader, the president of the board of directors of the DC Cooperative Housing Coalition, and Katie Wilson, the vice-president of the board, for their valuable editorial assistance. A thank-you also goes out to Janet Hulstrand for her additional editorial help.

For her assistance at the library of the Historical Society of Washington, D.C., I am indebted to research services librarian Jessica Smith. I also want to thank the Martin Luther King Jr. Memorial D.C. Public Library and its wonderful Washingtoniana Collection. There, I was helped by special collections librarian Michelle Casto, who allowed me to go through the library's old vertical file of co-op material, a trove of information. In addition, I consulted a number of other books while collecting information for this book, and one volume does stand out as being special: *Best Addresses*, by James M. Goode, is a magnificent book on the apartment houses of

Washington, D.C., and is one recommended to anyone interested in the city's history.

I would like to send a big thank-you to Joyce Rhodes of the Edmund J. Flynn Company for her hospitality and for providing me access to the historical materials in her company's files. I am also grateful to Sharon Flynn Tobing of the Edmund J. Flynn family, as she gave me access to her family's documents. A thank-you also goes out to Keith Parsons of 1705 Lanier Place, Northwest, for providing me with copies of some of his co-op's original records. In addition, I would like to thank Bill Didden, resident manager at the Ontario Apartment House, which is also in Lanier Heights, for supplying me with useful materials and good conversation. I also appreciate the help that was given to me by many other Washington, D.C. cooperatives.

At the DC Cooperative Housing Coalition, the other members of its board of directors deserve a huge thank-you. These individuals include: secretary Art Leabman; treasurer Ray Olson; and directors Matt Buzby, Fred Dyda, Loretta Glaze Elliott, Andy Litsky, Janet Sten and Spring Worth. I would also certainly like to thank the coalition's legal counsel Joseph Douglass. All of these individuals assisted with this book and the city's 2020 co-op activities.

Finally, a sincere and happy thank-you goes to The History Press and its staff. I especially want to thank editors Kate Jenkins and Ashley Hill for their patient and helpful management of this book through to its completion. And I thank Matthew Gilmore, noted Washington historian and author, for his fine Foreword.

# INTRODUCTION

How did the year 1920 become so special in the history of housing cooperatives in Washington, D.C.?

It was after the end of the First World War that the model of the modern housing cooperative was first envisioned in the city and introduced into the local real estate market. Although it was built on previous models that had been experimented with since the late nineteenth century, it was in 1920 that the detailed configuration of a modern co-op as we now know it was laid out and introduced to the Washington, D.C. market. The innovations included both the organizational arrangements of a co-op and, most importantly, some sound financial guidelines.

What precisely is a housing cooperative? A co-op is a building that is owned by a housing cooperative corporation, which, in turn, is owned and controlled by the members of the cooperative, usually through a shareholder agreement. Each member's share of that ownership gives that person (or persons) the right to occupy a specific apartment within the building, or complex of buildings, which are operated and maintained by the co-op association for the benefit of its resident-members and, in the long term, for the healthy ongoing existence of the cooperative. The individuals also have a decision-making voting right in the association.

Today, all around the world, housing cooperatives are thriving. In the early twentieth century, Washington, D.C., along with New York and Chicago, embraced and developed the idea of multiunit housing cooperative living and, in doing so, set a model to follow for other American cities.

# MODERN COOPERATIVE HOUSING: AN IDEA BROUGHT HOME FROM THE WA R

The Allan E. Walker Real Estate Company was active in the District of Columbia in the early part of the twentieth century. Founded in 1905, this firm quickly became involved in the initial development of parts of the Brookland neighborhood in the northeastern quadrant of the city as well as other residential areas of the District.

Walker had also become interested in the novel idea of cooperative home ownership. His firm was the first to introduce the concept of being able to buy a home in a multiunit building with a shared ownership structure to District residents, and he did this in an advertised, open-market manner. Edmund J. Flynn, who was stationed in England during the First World War, observed such cooperative arrangements in England and taken a special interest in this innovative idea. When he learned of Walker's plans for developing co-ops, he joined his firm and enthusiastically helped champion the development of cooperative apartment ownership and refine many of its functional details. In 1920, he helped create and market the first group of housing cooperatives in the District and almost immediately became the leading cooperative realtor in the city, opening his own firm in 1922. For the next half century, the Edmund J. Flynn Company went on to develop and convert more than sixty market-rate cooperatives in the District of Columbia.

# A CENTURY OF COOPERATIVE LIVING IN WASHINGTON

Over the past one hundred years, most of the city's co-ops were developed within four fairly distinct periods. First were the busy years from 1920 until the deepening of the Great Depression in 1932. The second period of robust development took place in the years after World War II, when major U.S. cities were undergoing considerable change and were working to stabilize and redefine themselves. In the 1960s, co-op development was introduced to southwest Washington, D.C.; this decade also saw some famous co-op buildings, most notably the Watergate, built along the Potomac River. Finally, the twelve-year period after 1973, following the granting of "home rule" to the District by Congress, saw a new surge in co-op development. This was a time when Washington, D.C., was being reinvigorated with fresh

1870 Wyoming Avenue, Northwest, a stately and well-designed building from 1917 in the Kalorama Triangle neighborhood. In 1951, it was converted into a co-op. *Photograph by the author.*

ideas, fresh businesses and new construction. It was generally becoming a more desirable place to live, with energetic, younger individuals deciding to move to the city. This narrative covers Washington, D.C.'s co-ops within these time periods in a generally chronological manner—but not strictly so.

Cooperatives in Washington, D.C., encompass a variety of building types in a range of styles, from simple to grand. Many of them are full of historical and architectural significance. They range in size from containing as few as four units to containing as many as hundreds. Some are contained within a single multiunit building, while others comprise an entire complex of buildings. There are high-rise apartment buildings, garden-style apartments and detached houses. Some are situated along streets in densely built-up areas of the central city, and others are located in more open environments in the outer sections of the District and encompass many acres of land.

This book will focus on the regular market-rate type of co-op, since this was the form of multiunit development that blossomed with the plans of 1920. Other types of co-ops, such as limited-equity co-ops or investment-owner arrangements, are generally not being examined here—with a few exceptions where it is useful to look at how these alternate forms may have interacted with regular market-rate co-ops.

Throughout human history and in almost every place that communities have been built, groups of individuals have chosen to pool their resources and build shared structures—their homes—for both pragmatic and idealistic reasons. This tribute to the history of housing cooperatives in the District of Columbia over the past one hundred years will tell one part of that very big story.

# 1

# 1920–1923: A HOUSING COOPERATIVE MOVEMENT BEGINS AND IS WELL RECEIVED IN THE CITY

After the end of World War I, as the modern federal government expanded and became more firmly established, Washington, D.C., experienced significant growth in its permanent population, with an accompanying growth in all kinds of construction.

In the District, the convergence of several social and economic factors led to the emergence of the modern housing cooperative. Among these factors were a growing desire for home ownership; an interest in living in a convenient and up-to-date home, one perhaps not requiring a lot of exterior upkeep; an increasing number of urban residents who could afford to buy their own homes; and the desire to live in a neighborly, congenial urban community.

Among the city's wealthy residents, the idea of living in an apartment, albeit an impressive, luxurious apartment, also became an increasingly attractive choice around this time. Previously, to the wealthy, apartment living had been considered something more appropriate for the working and middle classes. However, just before the turn of the twentieth century, among the upper levels of New York society, a luxury housing market had begun to develop. A small number of experienced real estate planners built several elaborate housing cooperatives in New York between 1890 and 1915 for this market. These were large, well-crafted homes in shared buildings that were sold to the very affluent, with many of these luxury apartments costing as much as a townhouse.

By the early 1920s, the trend had taken hold in Washington, D.C., as well, and some quite sumptuous apartment buildings were built. The 1920s became a booming period for new apartment housing construction in general, with buildings being created for all levels of society. In fact, it has been estimated that there were more apartment homes built in Washington, D.C., during the 1920s than single-family residences. By then, Washington, D.C., ranked among New York and Chicago as one of the cities with the largest percentage of apartment residents among their citizenry.

During this period, District planners were laying out and managing the growing city with deliberation. Zoning laws evolved, and roads were arranged. Many of the larger apartment-house structures were guided by city officials to be built primarily along major city thoroughfares, such as Connecticut and Massachusetts Avenues, lending their gracious exteriors to the growing urban landscape.

The exterior designs of many of the apartment houses in Washington, D.C., during this time were evolving from the rather formal Classical Revival style, which had been in fashion since the 1890s, into the more domestic English Revival style. This more-welcoming style often took on a Tudor Revival or Georgian look, mirroring what was beginning to be used for the exterior of many single-family homes in the 1920s and 1930s.

Meanwhile, the burgeoning cooperative movement was also becoming broadly accepted in New York, especially among the very affluent but also among the middle class. And in Chicago, a newly prosperous city of active people, cooperatives were also flourishing. During these years, the cooperative apartment movement in the United States was being crafted and defined in these three key cities. Later, the concept spread and, many times, was tried out in other parts of the country.

## EARLY FORMS OF CO-OP LIVING

To understand why cooperative housing grew to be a popular form of living in the United States in general—and in Washington, D.C., in particular—a brief bit of background is in order. The basic concept of cooperative housing is truly ancient and was very much a part of organized life in most of humanity's first city-communities. Going back to early historic times, in almost every culture all over the globe, people learned to coexist together in communities and to build homes together for many of the same reasons we do today. In ancient Rome, the *Digest of Justinian* describes cases of separate and legal home ownerships within a larger structure but with the shared possession of

Many years ago, castle living evolved as a way of providing the residents of each structure with a usually secure and agreeable home. Pictured: Arundel Castle in England. *Courtesy of the Library of Congress.*

a common roof. Shared proprietorship then, as now, was important because it created a beneficially vested self-interest among the individuals who were involved by establishing a mutual concern for having the property be correctly built and properly maintained. The early castles of Europe can also be said to have functioned as cooperatives. In fact, today, Kensington Palace is sometimes referred to as a co-op for the royal family.

The famous English worker co-ops of the mid-1800s established some basic patterns and had several origins, ranging from the progressively inspired projects of self-improvement groups to cases of enlightened business owners seeing the benefits of providing decent housing for their employees. The result from work on both sides was better housing for people. Robert Owen, a Welsh businessman, is regarded by many to be the father of the modern cooperative movement. Owen, who made his fortune in the production of cotton textiles, believed in the idea that decent housing and proper education for his workers were good for not only them but also for his business and society in general. He successfully put his forward-thinking concepts into practice at his cotton mills in Scotland. The housing at that locale became one of the models for the modern co-op. (A further look at the older history of co-ops is continued in chapter 9.)

In the latter half of the 1800s, a number of housing cooperatives were organized and built in the United States. Some were built by unions for their members, a concept that continued into the twentieth century, especially in and around New York City. In 1927, the Amalgamated Clothing Workers of America constructed its first cooperative, the 303-unit Amalgamated Cooperative Apartments, adjacent to the Van Cortlandt Park in the Bronx. In the late 1960s, the union-built Co-op City, one of the largest cooperatives in the United States, was also located in the Bronx. Today, this complex is home to more than fifteen thousand residents in thirty-five high-rise buildings and townhouses. There were other predecessors to the modern co-op as well—for instance, those arranged and built by religious or utopian communities.

As the modern urban environment developed in Washington, D.C., the usefulness of multi-unit rental apartment buildings quickly became clear, and they continued to proliferate throughout the city. Although discussion and

2852 Ontario Road, Northwest, one of Washington's earliest housing cooperatives. This is a quiet building in Adams Morgan. *Photograph by the author.*

debate about the desirability of apartment living continued for some time, eventually the idea became universally accepted as a sound economic model and a practical way of creating comfortable homes for urban residents.

In Washington, D.C., several buildings have been cited as the first—or among the first—of the city's housing cooperatives. One building with a solid claim to this first-place position was the Concord Apartments, which was built at New Hampshire Avenue and Swann Street, Northwest, in 1891. The Concord was a successful evolutionary apartment house design concept, but the economic depression of 1893 halted further explorations of the co-op idea. In 1962, the Concord was demolished as the area became more densely developed. Another very early co-op apartment building is located at 2852 Ontario Road, Northwest, in Lanier Heights. Built in 1909 as a co-op by six acquaintances who each wanted a solid, socially presentable and cost-effective home, this quiet, stylish brick building is sometimes cited as being the second cooperative in Washington, D.C., and now has a long history as a co-op. The original owners named it the Carrollton. With its sedate Arts and Crafts design, the building has a pleasant residential "feel" that befits the neighborhood. This style, as well as the related English Victorian home style, were popular designs that were used for some of the co-ops built in the 1920s.

## A First Step: The Conversion of Rental Apartments to Co-ops

In Washington, D.C., the first major wave of the city's modern housing co-ops consisted of the conversions of ten existing rental apartment buildings to apartments that were to be owned by their residents. These properties were solid, attractive and recently built structures that featured all of the up-to-date domestic conveniences and were created to house D.C.'s growing middle class. These conveniences included the latest plumbing designs and fixtures, newly developed electric lighting, telephones and, in some cases, elevators.

The people who were drawn to the co-ops included government workers; mid-level or upper mid-level employees of the city's private businesses; some military men and their families; and other professionals. In 1920, the

Allan E. Walker firm arranged the selection and creation of these ten initial cooperatives, with Edmund J. Flynn soon joining the firm to work on the details of the conversions and sales. On Saturday, March 27, the sales of apartments within the first of these co-op buildings were officially announced with major advertisements in the city's newspapers. The very first building to be converted was the Hoyt in the Columbia Heights neighborhood in Northwest. It was a fittingly typical representative of this initial group of apartment building conversions.

## THE HOYT

The Hoyt, the first of the initial ten apartment buildings that were converted to cooperative ownership in 1920. *Sketch from a 1921 promotional sales brochure, courtesy of the Edmund J. Flynn Company.*

A three-story Spanish Mission–style building at 1330 Belmont Street, Northwest, the Hoyt was completed in 1909 as the Columbia Heights neighborhood was first being built out. Sadly, it no longer exists, as it was razed at the end of the twentieth century after a period of decline. (A condo from 2009 now occupies its site.) But in its prime, the Hoyt was an attractive nine-unit building, with three generously sized apartments on each floor. The building was named for Alfred M. Hoyt, a New York investor who, along with Senator John Sherman in the late 1800s, had purchased a sizeable tract of land north of Florida Avenue. This area was then subdivided and became the southern portion of today's Columbia Heights.

According to the original plan for the Hoyt conversion, the apartments were first offered to the building's tenant-residents, with the remaining units being placed for sale on the open market. A look at three of those individuals who chose the Hoyt to be their home, as recorded in the 1920 D.C. City Directory, shows a good cross-section of the District's population. They were J. Lynn Yeagle, a newspaper editor; Olive E. Mills, a private secretary; and Harvey C. Pierce, a clerk at the Treasury Department.

With the successful sale of the Hoyt, the new housing co-op plans were off and running.

# The Co-op Developers: Allan E. Walker and Edmund J. Flynn

Today, the name of Edmund J. Flynn is synonymous with housing cooperatives in Washington, D.C., and it has been since 1920, when the modern financial structure of co-op ownership was introduced by the Allan E. Walker Company, with the young Flynn soon being associated with the real estate firm.

## Allan E. Walker

Allan Elliott Walker was born in the District on May 25, 1880, and was a noted—if only for a brief time—Washington, D.C. realtor and developer. In the 1890s, his father, Redford Walker, had also been a realtor in the burgeoning city. In addition to his real estate work, Allan Walker was a director of a local bank, the Continental Trust Company.

The Allan E. Walker Company Firm was active in the District and was involved in the development of several residential areas of the city. Walker, an industrious real estate developer who had fairly broad interests, enjoyed good business connections within the city. In 1922, these connections enabled him to start working on a major project, the design and construction of the renowned Mayflower Hotel on Connecticut Avenue. That large project, originally named the Hotel Walker, grew into a complex undertaking with many difficult aspects—financial, legal and structural—that evidently took a lot of managerial energy from the company.

In 1920, the firm also became actively interested in the idea of cooperative home ownership. It is remembered as the first to introduce this deliberately planned concept—that is, the concept of being able to buy a home in a multi-home building with a shared ownership of the structure—to District residents with a general, open-marketing program. And they introduced the idea that individuals would able to do this in essentially the same manner that they might buy a single-family home. At the time, Edmund J. Flynn was a young sales agent who had taken a special interest in this promising co-op idea and later worked on further refining many of the concept's functional details. Thus, auspiciously, in 1920, the firm marketed the first group of ten housing cooperatives in the District of Columbia. Flynn soon left the Walker Firm to establish his own real estate company that specialized in cooperatives.

Unfortunately, as the Mayflower Hotel project moved forward, construction difficulties and cost overruns compelled the Walker Firm to sell the project, in 1924, to the C.C. Mitchell Company. This new firm then completed the hotel and opened it in early 1925 under a new name, The Mayflower. Just a few months later, on May 14, 1925, Allan Walker died unexpectedly of a heart attack at the young age of forty-five, and the Walker Firm soon faded.

The development of the co-op concept then moved to Flynn.

## EDMUND J. FLYNN

Edmund Joseph Flynn, when he learned of Allan Walker's plans for co-ops, joined Walker's firm, and with enthusiasm, he championed the development of cooperative apartment ownership. Flynn almost immediately became the leading cooperative specialist and cooperative realtor in Washington, D.C., and he was able to open his own firm in 1922. The Edmund J. Flynn Company has developed or converted several dozen market-rate cooperatives in the District. The firm has been instrumental in creating a majority of the luxury cooperatives in the city as well as initiating, or assisting with, most of the District's solidly middle-class co-op buildings.

Flynn was born on February 13, 1889, just outside of St. Louis, to a newspaper family—his father published newspapers in southern Missouri. In 1919, he married Elsie Clohan, and they had two children, Edmund C. and Patricia. Edmund J. joined the navy in 1911, and he served in England during World War I. While he was there, he saw the housing cooperatives that were then being established. Regarding the co-ops, he later said this during an interview conducted for an article printed in the October 20, 1957 edition of the *Washington Post*:

> *I had seen* [co-ops] *in England and in New York, and it occurred to me that Washington presented a wonderful opportunity. We had a reservoir of government workers who were on the economic level of industrial workers. But the comparison ended there. Most of them were cultivated people. Cooperative apartments would provide them with nice homes at a price they could afford.*

Flynn employed a very successful model for new co-op development that he and Allan Walker had studied and developed. They would first plan the co-op's financial organization, then work on the marketing, executing the sales while the property developer worked on the structure's design, financing the initial construction and completing the actual construction. In most cases, the cooperatives were aimed at the upper middle class—individuals and families who wanted to live in the city with all its conveniences. But this procedure also included some properties that were created as luxury buildings.

Edmund J. Flynn, a well-regarded and active advocate of housing co-ops in Washington. *Courtesy of the Edmund J. Flynn Company.*

After his start in the 1920s and into the early 1930s, Flynn focused much of his efforts on buildings that were being planned for newly developing neighborhoods, most of which were located in the city's northwest quadrant.

Flynn wrote in *The Evolution of Cooperative Apartments*, one of his company brochures, "Co-operative apartment development affords the most economical home possible to obtain because of the advantage of collective buying power…the individuals pay only a small proportion of the cost of operation, and all enjoy the great benefits of the more luxurious building services." He explained that the estimated cost of operation for an individual owner of a cooperative apartment in a moderately sized apartment building was about 25 percent less than the cost of operating the same amount of floor space in a single-family house and added, "The larger the development, the lower the proportionate cost."

One favorable aspect of his work was his positive attitude. Edmund Flynn deeply believed in the social value of co-ops, noting (in the same brochure) that it was, in his opinion, "The best opportunity to do something constructive to meet a real human need for providing desirable homes for a large class of people who are burdened with heavy rental payments and have little or no hope of satisfying the inherent desire of everyone to own his own home."

Flynn's leadership and his accomplishments in the field allowed him to quickly become one of the nation's foremost authorities on co-op housing. His "100 Percent Co-operative Plan" served as the model for cooperatives in many other parts of the country and permitted almost all of his early developments to weather the various economic ups-and-downs of the twentieth century. His hands-on approach and his upbeat attitude were likely also important components that contributed to the successful creation

The Flynns, father and son Edmund J. and Edmund C., during World War II. Their company was the major facilitator of co-op development in Washington, D.C. *Courtesy of the Flynn family.*

of the majority of his projects, and they surely helped with the routinely positive image that co-ops soon acquired. Flynn was also very aware of the power of advertising and became skilled at creating well-placed newspaper advertisements and pieces that promoted his projects.

While working on the cooperatives of Washington, D.C., Edmund, along with his family, chose to live in some of his developments after they were completed. This included the newly constructed Hampshire Gardens block in Petworth and, later, the Presidential on Sixteenth Street, Northwest, after it was converted. Additionally, he was instrumental in the development of a number of co-op projects outside of Washington, D.C., notably in Maryland and Florida. Edmund J. Flynn died on May 28, 1983, in New York City.

The firm that Flynn created, from its very beginning, was a central point for the handling of cooperative share transfers, and it was a clearinghouse for information about D.C. co-ops. Today, the Edmund J. Flynn Company is still the repository of almost all of the share records of the cooperatives of Washington, D.C., and its suburbs. Edmund Flynn also lobbied on behalf of co-ops, both nationwide and locally. For example, he notably proposed early on that political and civic officials across the nation should consider selling apartments to the disadvantaged, rather than simply providing them with rental units. In our modern society, these broad ideas for housing co-ops in their various forms continue to be discussed and explored.

After the end of World War II, Edmund J.'s son, Edmund C., entered the business and helped to carry on his father's tradition. The younger Flynn was born in 1923 and died in Washington, D.C., in 2008. The company had been sold in 1984 to Bill Karas, a longtime employee of the firm. More recently, in 2016, the ownership of the company was passed along and sold to another long-term employee, Joyce Rhodes, who kept it as a locally owned enterprise. Today, the Edmund J. Flynn Company is an important city resource and a hub in the world of cooperative real estate in Washington, D.C., and it continues to maintain its close association with D.C.-area co-ops.

## Further information about the Initial Ten Cooperative Conversions

In March 1921, the Allan E. Walker firm decided to publish a brochure to celebrate its successful first year of cooperative housing activities. The brochure included an excerpt from a *Washington Post* article from December 1920 titled "Laud Cooperative Apartment Homes." Subheadings summarized the story: "Stockholders of Eight Corporations Report

The cover of the 1921 Allan E. Walker sales brochure, which was produced to extol the benefits of cooperative living. *Courtesy of the Edmund J. Flynn Company.*

Experiment Is Working Out Satisfactorily," "Model for the Neighborhood" and "Proud of Home Ownership."

The 100-percent co-op financial plan was a key feature that Allan E. Walker and Edmund Flynn worked out early on. This financial model was used for each of their projects and required a sufficient and necessary down payment—usually 20 percent. Properties had to be sold as entirely cooperatively owned and were usually owner-occupied. This provided their co-ops with the invested self-interest and the stability that was needed for long-term success.

The ten apartment houses that were listed in the brochure, all sturdy up-to-date buildings, were quickly sold. In the order of their formations, they were: the Hoyt, Dumbarton Court, the Adelphia, the Netherlands, the Cavanaugh, the Avondale, the Stafford, the Parkwood, Rutland Courts and the Lambert. Three of these buildings had been built by Harry Wardman (the Avondale, the Cavanaugh and Rutland Courts), and three of them had been built by Bates Warren (the Lambert, the Netherlands and the Stafford). These two developers continued to remain connected to the new co-op construction that soon occurred in Washington, D.C.

Happily, most of these early co-op conversions are still familiar names today, and they continue to thrive as cooperatives. After the conversion of the Hoyt, the others that followed—that now remain—are reviewed in the following sections. Two are not covered: the Parkwood at Eighteenth and K Streets downtown, which was razed and replaced by a large office building as K Street dramatically evolved, and the Adelphia at Fourteenth and Chapin Streets, Northwest, which reverted to being a rental building as its neighborhood became, over time, less desirable to homeowners.

## DUMBARTON COURT

In mid-1920, the very attractive Dumbarton Court Apartment Building at 1657 Thirty-First Street, Northwest, was converted, and its apartments were sold. Situated right in the heart of Georgetown, this building, originally completed with thirty-five units in 1910, had been designed, developed and built by architect George S. Cooper. The fact that Cooper had held onto the property as an investment for himself likely made the sale and transition to ownership by the residents more possible. It is reasonable to think that the architect would have been happy to have his fine structure cared for by owners. There are currently twenty-seven units in Dumbarton Court, down from the initial thirty-five. This change in the number of units serves as a good example of the often-fluid nature of co-op apartment share transitions. Sometimes, units are combined, and sometimes, larger ones are split into two.

## THE CAVANAUGH

This co-op is now named Cavanaugh Court, and it is another one of the well-made buildings that was developed and built by the legendary Harry Wardman. It is located at 1526 Seventeenth Street, Northwest, in the DuPont Circle neighborhood, and it was built in 1916. Designed with four floors by noted architect Albert M. Schneider, it now has fifty-two co-op apartments. This pleasant Georgian-style structure is a solid neighborhood element at the corner of Seventeenth and Church Streets, Northwest.

## RUTLAND COURTS

Rutland Courts, a Harry Wardman building, was among the first ten apartment houses to be converted into a co-op. *Image from the 1921 promotional brochure, courtesy of the Edmund J. Flynn Company.*

Rutland Courts at 1726 Seventeenth Street, Northwest, is another brick apartment building that was constructed in 1917 by developer Harry Wardman in an attractive Classical Revival style. As one of the original ten co-ops, the building has a long and proud cooperative history. Today, it remains a comfortable five-story home for its members, with a nice roof deck that offers excellent city views. Rutland Courts is conveniently situated just east of DuPont Circle. It contains seventy-nine apartments.

## THE NETHERLANDS

This fine cooperative, a well-crafted building at 1852 Columbia Road in Adams Morgan, was created by Bates Warren in 1909. The Netherlands was solidly constructed of brick and stone in a Classical Revival style with good detailing, and it was designed by architects Hunter and Bell. It has six floors, with five apartments on each floor. After it became a co-op—using the "100 Percent Co-op" financial plan—it was held aloft as a successful example of this new type of real estate ownership. The building is well located on Columbia Road in the Washington Heights area.

## THE STAFFORD AND THE LAMBERT

These two coordinating but visually different buildings sit next each other at 1789 and 1791 Lanier Place in Northwest and were built just one year apart. The Stafford, at 1789 Lanier Place, was created first in 1911. Both were developed by William H. Sholes, a lawyer in the office of developer Bates Warren. On the completion of the two, Sholes kept possession of the Lambert and made his home there in a large apartment. He handed the ownership of the Stafford over to Bates Warren, who had provided the financing and, apparently, much of the construction expertise needed

---announcing:

**Corporation**
Is Completed for
**Cooperative Ownership**
OF
**The Lambert Apartments**
**1791 Lanier Place**

which marks the practical completion of the sale of the tenth apartment building in Washington, sold under the

**WALKER PLAN OF COOPERATIVE OWNERSHIP**

Cooperative ownership is no longer an experiment in Washington. It is a conspicuous, proven success, even more so than in other cities, because of the improvements and refinements effected in the drafting of the WALKER PLAN.

Cooperative apartments have blazed a new trail to home satisfaction. Ask any of the great number of purchasers. Apartments in charge of cooperative owners become a better place to live in. They are better operated and residence therein is eminently more satisfactory.

**YOU CAN BUY AN APARTMENT**
in This Splendid Building That Will Be Your Very Own for a

SMALL CASH PAYMENT AND MONTHLY PAYMENTS LOWER THAN YOU ARE PAYING AS RENT. BE DONE WITH RENT RECEIPTS AND TAKE THIS SHORT CUT TO OWNERSHIP.

**Most Lambert Apartments Are Already Sold**
**A Choice Few Remain**
Do Not Delay Action as This Is the Last Opportunity to Offer at a Figure 40 Per Cent Less Than Reproduction Cost.

**Apartments in THE LAMBERT Sell as Follows:**

3 Rooms, Bath and Porch, $4,300 and $4,500. Cash payments, $1,400 to $1,500. Total monthly payments, $41.04 to $42.60*.

5 Rooms, Bath and Porch, $7,400. Cash payment, $2,500. Total monthly payment, $69.72*.

4 Rooms, Bath and Porch, $5,500 to $6,000. Cash payments, $1,800 to $2,000. Total monthly payments, $52.40 to $56.80*.

8 Rooms, 2 Baths and Porch, $12,000. Cash payment, $4,000. Total monthly payment, $113.60*.

*The monthly payments above INCLUDE your proportionate share of taxes, heat, water, light, janitor service and similar expenses, all interest and a substantial curtail on the principal.

**Allan E. Walker & Co., Inc.**
Originators of the Perfected Cooperative Plan in Washington
813 Fifteenth Street — Southern Building

An advertisement for the Lambert Co-op in the June 12, 1921 edition of the *Washington Post. Courtesy of the Lambert Owners Cooperative.*

for the creation of the two structures. Both were proficiently designed by architects Hunter and Bell, and both have four floors each. The Lambert has seventeen units, and the Stafford contains sixteen. The two buildings blend in well with the other properties on their friendly city street.

Finally, the Avondale is a somewhat unusual case. It became a co-op and then, twenty years later, was sold to an investor and reverted to being a rental property. Several years after that event, it again became a co-op. The Avondale is examined ahead, on page 75.

# THE ARCHITECTS

The architects of Washington, D.C.'s cooperatives made up a diverse group of designers. They ranged from individuals in small practices to notable architects, busy maestros with large, prolific firms. Working within a range of styles, they created a large number of memorable structures. Highlighted in boxes in the text ahead are some of the more prominent architects who are responsible for many of the District's co-op buildings. There is certainly no intention to slight those individuals who are not highlighted here, as they, too, created some truly special structures. A more complete list of co-op architects and the buildings with which they are associated is contained in the reference tables at the end of the book.

The following three architects and their design firms were responsible for creating a good number of the early buildings that were converted into co-ops after the buildings had been constructed and established.

**George S. Cooper** (1864–1929) was a native Washingtonian who became an influential local architect, builder and developer. During his forty-year career, he designed single-family dwellings and office buildings, but he was most well known for his apartment designs. For a time, Cooper worked for the noted Hornblower & Marshall Firm. Eventually, as an independent architect, he designed a large number of structures throughout the D.C. area, including twenty-four apartment buildings between 1892 and 1909. He also designed the noteworthy Bond Building, an office building on Fourteenth Street, Northwest, near the White House.

Today, Cooper is especially remembered for crafting efficient floor plans in the apartments he designed. *History of the City of Washington,* published in 1903, noted, "No young man has played a more important part in the active growth and great development of Greater Washington than George S. Cooper." Over the course of his career, he was responsible for designing around 850 properties, including homes, commercial buildings and apartments, several of which are listed in the National Register of Historic Places.

Although he was not the first to design apartment buildings in Washington, D.C., Cooper played a major role in popularizing their acceptance. His work encouraged middle-class citizens to reconsider the changing urban environment and to no longer see apartment buildings as being only for the upper class or the lower class. He was also the first local architect to reduce design costs by replicating plans for apartment buildings, a practice that became very popular in late nineteenth and early twentieth centuries. His first ventures of this kind, the Gladstone and the Hawarden, were the first documented "twin" apartment buildings in the city. His last apartment building was Dumbarton Court.

**Hunter & Bell**. This architectural firm was active in Washington, D.C., primarily in the north-central areas of the city, during the early years of the twentieth century, when the neighborhoods there were being established. Architects Ernest C. Hunter (1881–1945) and G. (George) Neal Bell (1879–1956) both grew up in Washington, D.C. Their firm was formed in 1902 and continued operations until 1918. Quite prolific, they created roughly eight hundred buildings, mostly in the Adams Morgan, Mount Pleasant, Columbia Heights and Bloomingdale neighborhoods.

Hunter and Bell left behind a fine legacy of handsome, solid structures. They designed row houses, single-family homes and apartment houses, as well as some commercial properties in a variety of styles, but they very often used the Classical Revival motif. Their work ranged from modest middle-class to top-level luxury buildings. Although their façades were usually done in a traditional style, they generally planned their structures using the most modern of construction techniques. Almost all of their larger buildings were made of brick and a reinforced concrete interior, which was, at that time, a relatively new construction method. Hunter and Bell designed several of the buildings that are now D.C. cooperatives. The advent of World War I ended the partnership, as Hunter was disabled during his war service.

**Albert H. Beers** (1859–1911) began his professional career in Bridgeport, Connecticut, in 1886. Although he only practiced in Washington, D.C., for a brief period, he had a significant effect on the development of the city. Beers was an extremely prolific designer, mainly due to his employment as chief architect at Harry Wardman. In this role, Beers designed approximately one thousand dwellings between 1905 and 1911. Locally, he was credited with putting forward the idea of the front-porch row house design, which became very popular in many District neighborhoods.

Importantly, he designed more than seventy apartment buildings for Harry Wardman, including the Northumberland; almost all of these were sturdy brick structures. Beers additionally created buildings for other city developers. He also designed Wardman's own home in 1909, a noteworthy Spanish-style house in the Woodley Park neighborhood. Beers died unexpectedly in 1911 at the age of fifty-two.

## SEPARATE EARLY CONVERSIONS

Around 1920, the District was experiencing a series of major rent increases, and residents in a small number of the top-level luxury buildings were therefore looking into the idea of cooperative ownership as a way of stabilizing their housing costs and investing in real estate. This ownership would also permit them to be able to exercise greater control within their neighborhoods. Thus, a few of the buildings that remain today as notable high-end co-ops were self-converted by the people who were already living in them.

## THE NORTHUMBERLAND

In the Dupont Circle neighborhood, the distinctive Northumberland Cooperative is one such example of the then-present renters converting their building into co-op. This building at 2039 New Hampshire Avenue, Northwest, was constructed in 1910 by Harry Wardman and designed by

The Northumberland Apartments

(Co-operative Company)

New Hampshire Avenue and V Street

Our Co-operative Plan

Entire capital stock of "Northumberland Apartments, Inc.," is divided in blocks representing prices of each apartment.

Ownership of stock represents ownership of apartment.

Each stockholder pays share of general expenses represented by his proportion of stock—as liberally assessed for first year this is $3.75 monthly for each $1,000 of stock.

Former owners of building retain ownership of stock unsold, receive rents and pay assessments for expenses on apartments unsold.

Purchasers commence from date their purchase is made—there is no deficit—merely the substitution of one stockholder for another with all charges paid to date.

The company now owns and operates the property. Immediate possession can be given of several desirable apartments, and arrangements are being made for future vacancies. Why pay high apartment rents when you can pay your share of actual cost?

Mr. Seay on premises daily, 4 to 8 o'clock;

Sunday, 10 to 8 o'clock.

For information and floor plans apply to

Union Realty Corporation, Agents

910 Evans Building Main 8415

*Top*: The prominent Northumberland Apartment House, located in the Dupont Circle neighborhood, from about 1920. *Courtesy of the Library of Congress.*

*Bottom*: A newspaper advertisement announcing the new cooperative at the Northumberland Apartments. *Courtesy of the* Washington Times, *March 26, 1921.*

one of his best architects, Albert H. Beers (noted earlier). Originally opened as a luxury apartment house, the Northumberland quickly became home to many prominent members of Washington, D.C.'s society, including several members of Congress and some of the local wealthy elite, a group that also included people of the city's growing merchant class. This seven-story Classical Revival building is distinguished by its elegant lobby and detailed brick exterior; it now contains sixty-seven apartments in a variety of sizes. The building was formally converted into a cooperative in 1920 and is the oldest continuously self-managed cooperative building in the city. Today, the interior of the building retains its fine lobby, dramatic staircase and spacious apartments.

On October 10, 1920, the *Washington Post* reported on the sale of the Northumberland.

> *The sale of the Northumberland apartments, New Hampshire Avenue and V Street Northwest, to the "Northumberland Apartments, Inc." has been announced by the Union Realty Corporation, Evans building. The purchasing company will dispose of individual apartments on the cooperative plan. C.C. Calhoun and James Sharp made the sale.*
>
> *The Northumberland is a seven-story, modern, fireproof building, containing 69 apartments, varying in size from two to seven rooms. It was built about nine years ago.*

AS THE SALES OF cooperatives progressed, several other local real estate firms, along with some innovative property owners, took note of the success of the concept and also created cooperatives from existing apartment rental stock. Most of these were well-planned projects with good, solid buildings, but a few were apparently arranged without enough forethought and did not last as co-ops in the long run. Such structures were usually returned to the market as rental properties, especially when tougher economic times came. Flynn's requirements that there be adequate down payments and that the property be 100 percent cooperatively owned were certainly important central elements. These were quickly seen to be necessary for establishing a co-op with stability and a healthy future.

Practical social issues were also matters that needed to be considered. During the late nineteenth century, there were the small number of apartment buildings created with what could be called cooperative ownership, but this ownership was usually a unique or custom-created situation. These situations included: having a few individual friends or acquaintances joining to create a shared ownership or a developer constructing a building for friends with the specific intention of selling the apartments to them. The famous Hay-Adams House, built in 1885 on H Street and Sixteenth Street, Northwest, was such a jointly owned structure. The families of John Hay, President Lincoln's secretary, and noted writer Henry Adams were close friends, and the men and their wives split the construction costs and shared the ownership of this building.

Such early creations produced some useful and realistic knowledge about the kinds of issues that could arise in a shared-living situation within a larger building, especially with an ongoing co-ownership. Consequently, when the contemporary cooperative concept arose, real-life operational considerations, such as the importance of a basic level of mutual compatibility and having practical, established ground rules, were understood. These matters were then able to be thought through and addressed with some useful, common-sense planning.

# 2

# 1924–1940: COOPERATIVES FLOURISH WITH NEW CONSTRUCTION BUT ARE SLOWED BY THE GREAT DEPRESSION

## A Large Second Step: New Construction of Purposely Built Cooperatives

With the success of rental apartment buildings being converted into multi-owner homes, the major planners of this modern concept quickly became busy laying out and creating buildings designed from the start as cooperatives. During this time, the city had only a fairly small group of local developers who specialized in creating multiunit rental apartment housing. It appears that just about all of them looked with interest at this new idea of co-ops. Often, the regular model for developing and creating an apartment house at that time was that a developer would construct a property and then, right away, would sell the completed building to another investor. This method of development seems to have fit in nicely with the creation of a cooperatively owned structure. The developer could still make money and create a further demand for new homes in their projects.

Thus, a few builders actively embraced the co-op idea, deeming it good for the city, for co-op residents and, of course, for themselves. As it turns out, many of the larger developers who were then active in Washington, D.C., at least tried out the co-op concept with one or two buildings. The growing city also created suitable conditions for this ownership plan. But there was one family of developers who brought cooperative housing properties to Washington, D.C., in a notable way. This family, the Warrens, created many fine homes, and they will be the first builders examined from this period.

# The Warren Family

This group of developers and builders had a significant and beneficial effect on all types of housing in Washington, D.C., during the first half of the twentieth century. Their early well-constructed buildings helped to create the neighborhoods of Adams Morgan, Mount Pleasant and Columbia Heights. They also worked in many other city neighborhoods as the District continued to be built-out and expanded.

The first generation of the family in D.C. were two brothers, Bates Warren and John L. Warren. The brothers were born and raised in Alabama, and both had studied law before settling in the District around 1895. They rather quickly jumped into the world of real estate development, which, at the time, was mainly composed of a fairly small group of local residents. Their family was comfortable but not wealthy. However, private money was then flowing into Washington, D.C. (from activities around the nation), and Bates, especially, appears to have been successfully adept at tapping into this new pool of investment capital that was available. With his local banking connections—he had become vice president of a small bank, the Continental Trust Company—and his friendships with some of the wealthier D.C. residents, Bates apparently crafted a reliable source of funding. In particular, he became friends with prominent senator Francis E. Warren of Wyoming, the remarkably moneyed and famous founder of Cheyenne, Wyoming. With energy, these two Warren brothers created many structures in D.C. and later encouraged their two more well-known nephews to do likewise. The two, Monroe and R. Bates Warren, had a very large effect on the early growth of housing cooperatives in D.C.

**Bates Warren** (1869–1940), in addition to being a busy real estate developer, worked as a prominent Washington real estate lawyer. In the District, he was responsible for the planning and construction of dozens of attractive apartment houses in the mid-city neighborhoods, including those in areas just north of the original older city, when those neighborhoods were being built out. During the time that he was active in developing properties, starting around 1902, Bates became friends with many of the other developers who were then active in the real estate community and the local business world. His interest in sound city growth seems to have had a positive effect on his nephews, especially on Monroe Warren, who had come to work for Bates just as he was creating some of his finest buildings.

**John L. Warren** (1872–1921) fashioned some superior buildings in the near-northwest areas of the city; several of these were subsequently converted by E.J. Flynn into co-ops. John used the same architectural firm, Hunter & Bell, as the more prolific Bates, and they also usually worked with the same construction firms. Both John and Bates Warren also worked with respected civil engineer Carroll Beale, who guided them in their use of internal reinforced concrete constructions, a building method that, at the time, was fairly new. This engineering work helped set the standards for the subsequent use of reinforced concrete, first in the Washington area and then nationally.

At first, Bates and John L. Warren worked together, but soon, they went on to operate separately, usually in the same neighborhoods, and sometimes even within the same block, building single-family homes and apartment houses. One of the first large structures they developed was the Alabama, a seven-story building that was erected in 1905 in downtown Washington, D.C., at 1015 N Street, Northwest. The building had an unusual history.

When the Alabama opened, it was a prestigious but standard apartment building. However, in 1918, it was purchased by the C&P Telephone Co., which planned for it to become a convenient and secure residential building for its phone operators during World War I. C&P retained ownership of the building until 1922, when it was sold and converted into a co-op, but apparently, this occurred in a somewhat casual manner, one that may not have required much of a financial commitment from each of its individual members. This "cooperative without a home ownership commitment" was a co-op type that occurred as an alternative to the Flynn Plan (which required that members invest in owning their apartments). Often—as seen historically—these "cooperatives without financial home ownership commitments" were less likely to succeed, since the level of personal down-payment participation and obligation to the building was not as strong.

Nevertheless, the Alabama lasted as a co-op through the late 1950s, when the building reverted to being a regular rental property. Casual cooperatives such as this did exist in various city neighborhoods, starting around 1925, for several decades, and they usually either quickly became stabilized as genuine homeowner-occupied co-op properties or returned to being rental buildings.

The Alabama was a well-built brick-and-stone structure, but by the midcentury, the neighborhood around it had declined, and apparently, the building had also deteriorated. After it was purchased and razed around 1972, the land on which it sat became a parking lot.

# CO-OP DEVELOPERS: MONROE WARREN AND R. BATES WARREN

John and Bates Warren had another brother, Dr. Benjamin S. Warren, who had also moved to Washington, D.C., from Alabama to work as an assistant surgeon general. He later became an administrator in the U.S. Marine Corps Hospital Service and was instrumental in the creation of the U.S. Public Health Service. Benjamin settled in the District with his family, which included his two sons: Monroe (1895–1983) and Robert Bates (1897–1976).

Monroe had planned to follow in his father's footsteps and become a doctor, but his summer job working for his uncle Bates during college caused him to change his plans. He decided to instead enter the construction business, so he, along with R. Bates, founded the company M. & R.B. Warren Inc. in 1920.

When the two brothers were just starting out, in 1921, their first major building project was creating a fair number of solid bungalows and row houses in Northwest Washington, D.C. In 1922, the two moved into constructing multifamily structures and started with a relatively basic but attractive apartment house at 2525 Ontario Road, Northwest. They followed that with two more elaborate buildings in Lanier Heights. By 1923, they had moved into developing cooperative apartment buildings, most often working with the Edmund J. Flynn Company.

The buildings they crafted, which were primarily developed by Monroe Warren, became some of the more noted D.C. cooperatives of the 1920s. Monroe had a good eye for talent. He drew on some skilled but young and generally unestablished architects, and his developments benefited. While Monroe was busy planning projects and working on the construction end of the new co-op developments, his brother, R. Bates, was working on the organizational side of co-op advancement. By 1925, R. Bates had become the chairman of the Co-operative Apartment Division of the National Association of Real Estate Boards, which was then headquartered in Chicago. From that position, R. Bates Warren actively promoted co-ops by writing about them in both local and national publications.

Over the years, Monroe Warren, in particular, had a major effect on housing of all types throughout the Washington, D.C. area. After 1930, Monroe and R. Bates separated their businesses and went to work on their own real estate ventures. Monroe's first project without his brother was perhaps his most well known, the Kennedy-Warren Apartment Building at

3133 Connecticut Avenue, Northwest. For this massive project, he teamed up with another successful developer, Edgar S. Kennedy. The Kennedy-Warren was started in 1931, just as the Great Depression was taking hold. By 1932, only the main central portion of the building had been completed, and the project was forced into bankruptcy. It was then taken over by the lender, who then finished one of the wings in 1935.

But following this partial completion, the building did open and became the most prominent luxury Art Deco–style apartment building in Washington, D.C. In fact, at the time, it was known as the most architecturally significant modern apartment building in the city. Its exterior, with aluminum spandrels and limestone carvings, embodies the geometric characteristics of Art Deco in a dramatic manner. Seventy-four years later, in 2004, the last and especially large wing of the original design was finally completed. This new work finished the original plan of the building, matching the details of its original style and winning several national awards for the quality of its architecture and attention to historical construction detail. These awards included the 2005 Award of Excellence in Historic Resources from the American Institute of Architects.

After the Kennedy-Warren project went into bankruptcy, Monroe Warren returned to building single-family homes in residential neighborhoods. He started building the first of these types of housing developments in the nearby suburb of Chevy Chase, Maryland, in 1930. Called Meadowbrook, it consisted primarily of attractive two-story single-family homes. Later, he worked with the new Federal Housing Administration (FHA) to lay out housing standards for federally insured homes, and he also continued to work on home developments elsewhere in Maryland and Virginia. He contributed substantially to the growth of some of the residential neighborhoods around the greater Washington area. His final building project was the Woodley Gardens development in Rockville, Maryland.

Separately, R. Bates Warren also remained in the housing construction field, developing homes primarily in suburban Maryland. He also later worked as a real estate broker.

The following is an overview of the cooperative developments created by Monroe and R. Bates Warren up until 1930.

# 1705 Lanier Place, Northwest

This attractive four-story brick structure is generally considered to be the first modern property in Washington that was specifically planned and built as a housing cooperative. It was designed by architect James E. Cooper with a striking Old English Tudor–style exterior. The building is larger than it appears; it drops down a hillside in the rear, adding floors. In 1923, as the idea of creating this property was first being contemplated by the Warren Brothers, Flynn approached the two with the novel concept of selling the brand-new apartments as co-op homes. They agreed to the idea and commissioned Flynn to market and sell the co-op shares for the building while it was still under construction. He sold all of the unit shares before the construction was even complete, prompting the Warrens to partner with him on several upcoming projects.

The co-op's organizing documents and house rules were apparently set up with some good forethought. It also seems that its documents were used in part to set the subsequent standards that were used for the procedures and

1705 Lanier Place, in Lanier Heights. This building was the first modern project in Washington to be planned from the ground up as a co-op. *Photograph by the author.*

| | Apt. No. | Price | Cash | Monthly payment | Monthly assessment | Total monthly | Comparison with monthly rental value |
|---|---|---|---|---|---|---|---|
| Apartments with one bed room, living room, dining alcove, kitchen, reception hall, and bath. | 103 | $5,450 | $1,090 | $43.60 | $10.90 | $54.50 | $65.00 |
| | 4 | 4,900 | 980 | 39.20 | 9.80 | 49.00 | 60.00 |
| | 5 | 5,700 | 1,140 | 45.60 | 11.40 | 57.00 | 67.50 |
| | 6 | 5,450 | 1,090 | 43.60 | 10.90 | 54.50 | 65.00 |
| | 7 | 6,400 | 1,280 | 51.20 | 12.80 | 64.00 | 75.00 |
| | 201 | 5,900 | 1,180 | 47.20 | 11.80 | 59.00 | 70.00 |
| | 2 | 5,700 | 1,140 | 45.60 | 11.40 | 57.00 | 67.50 |
| | 3 | 5,900 | 1,180 | 47.20 | 11.80 | 59.00 | 70.00 |
| | 4 | 5,700 | 1,140 | 45.60 | 11.40 | 57.00 | 67.50 |
| | 5 | 5,900 | 1,180 | 47.20 | 11.80 | 59.00 | 70.00 |
| | 6 | 5,900 | 1,180 | 47.20 | 11.80 | 59.00 | 70.00 |
| | 7 | 6,400 | 1,280 | 51.20 | 12.80 | 64.00 | 75.00 |
| | 301 | 6,150 | 1,230 | 49.20 | 12.30 | 61.50 | 72.50 |
| | 3 | 5,900 | 1,180 | 47.20 | 11.80 | 59.00 | 70.00 |
| | 5 | 5,900 | 1,180 | 47.20 | 11.80 | 59.00 | 70.00 |
| | 7 | 6,400 | 1,[illegible]80 | 51.20 | 12.80 | 64.00 | 75.00 |
| | 401 | 6,150 | 1,230 | 49.20 | 12.30 | 61.50 | 72.50 |
| | 3 | 5,900 | 1,1[illegible]0 | 47.20 | 11.80 | 59.00 | 70.00 |
| | 5 | 5,900 | 1,180 | 47.20 | 11.80 | 59.00 | 70.00 |
| | 7 | 6,400 | 1,280 | 51.20 | 12.80 | 64.00 | 75.00 |
| Apartments with two bed rooms, etc. | 108 | 7,400 | 1,480 | 59.20 | 14.80 | 74.00 | 85.00 |
| | 208 | 7,400 | 1,480 | 59.20 | 14.80 | 74.00 | 85.00 |
| | 302 | 7,400 | 1,480 | 59.20 | 14.80 | 74.00 | 85.00 |
| | 4 | 7,400 | 1,480 | 59.20 | 14.80 | 74.00 | 85.00 |
| | 6 | 7,400 | 1,480 | 59.20 | 14.80 | 74.00 | 85.00 |
| | 8 | 7,400 | 1,480 | 59.20 | 14.80 | 74.00 | 85.00 |
| | 402 | 7,400 | 1,480 | 59.20 | 14.80 | 74.00 | 85.00 |
| | 4 | 7,400 | 1,480 | 59.20 | 14.80 | 74.00 | 85.00 |
| | 6 | 7,400 | 1,480 | 59.20 | 14.80 | 74.00 | 85.00 |
| | 8 | 7,400 | 1,480 | 59.20 | 14.80 | 74.00 | 85.00 |
| | | 192,000 | 38,400 | 1,536.00 | 384.00 | 1,920.00 | 2,247.50 |

ESTIMATED BUDGET FOR ONE YEAR

| | |
|---|---|
| Taxes | $1,000.00 |
| Janitor | 600.00 |
| Water rent | 125.00 |
| Management | 1,200.00 |
| Coal | 1,000.00 |
| Electricity | 100.00 |
| Insurance | 200.00 |
| Ashes | 125.00 |
| Supplies | 250.00 |
| | $4,600.00 |

From 1705 Lanier Place, Northwest, a page from the sales prospectus that shows some of the sales prices and anticipated costs of the new co-op. *Courtesy of the 1705 Lanier Place Co-op.*

policies in a number of co-ops that followed. For instance, the house rules at 1705 were sensibly drawn up but very soon evolved with modifications. At first, children were not allowed in the apartments of 1705, but this rule was reviewed and discontinued before long.

## *Projects Around Porter Street*

At the same time that the Warrens were starting the construction of 1705 Lanier Place, they were also planning additional apartment houses that were to be sold as co-ops, including a new set of six buildings known as the Cleveland Park Apartments from 3018 to 3028 Porter Street. These were matching structures that were situated on well-landscaped residential grounds, and their distinctive look very visibly announced that they were co-ops to Washington, D.C. residents. But before that set was built, the brothers' next two smaller projects were created.

These next two Warren brothers ventures, which were separate but built almost simultaneously, consisted of, at first, three attractive and solid buildings at 3407, 3409 and 3411 Twenty-Ninth Street, Northwest, followed by 3001 Porter Street, Northwest. This first set of three matching two-story buildings had a total of twenty-four units. They share in the distinction of being among the first deliberately built co-op properties in Washington, D.C. Located just south of Ordway Street, off of Connecticut Avenue, they were designed by architect G. Neal Bell (formerly of Hunter & Bell) in an orderly, formal Georgian style. They were completed in 1924.

The second structure, 3001 Porter Street, Northwest, was a stand-alone thirteen-unit brick building, and it was also completed in 1924. It was designed by James E. Cooper and has a striking Tudor Revival timber-frame exterior, similar to that of 1705 Lanier Place, Northwest.

## THE CLEVELAND PARK APARTMENTS

The Cleveland Park Apartments, located at 3018, 3020, 3022, 3024, 3026 and 3028 Porter Street, Northwest, were designed to fit in well with the upscale single-family homes that were then being built in Cleveland Park. In 1924, following the successful completion of 1705 Lanier Place, the Warren brothers planned this set of six three-story brick buildings as

3018 Porter Street, Northwest, under construction in 1925. One of the original buildings of the six Cleveland Park Apartments group. *Courtesy of the Edmund J. Flynn Company.*

*Left*: A contemporary advertisement for these new co-op apartments. Each building today is known by its Porter Street address. *Courtesy of the Edmund J. Flynn Company.*

*Right*: Another Flynn advertisement created to promote these new cooperatives. *Courtesy of the Edmund J. Flynn Company.*

the next step up in growth. Today, they serve as an effective example of smart medium-density urban housing. This group of buildings was initially known collectively as the Cleveland Park Apartments. Today, each separate building is a cooperative known by its individual Porter Street address. The architect for these buildings was James E. Cooper. The co-ops sit as a cohesive collection of buildings in their neighborhood. Designed in a Victorian Domestic English style, each building was built with twelve units. They are arrayed down the street on pleasant lawns, with parking provided in the rear of each of the buildings. Inside, they are fashioned with useful modern layouts. Their construction was completed in 1925

## 1661 CRESCENT PLACE

This five-story property just off of Sixteenth Street, Northwest, contains fifty-five apartments. It is a gracious, expansive structure that was designed by Joseph Younger, and its construction was started in 1925. Situated across from Meridian Hill Park, on the hill overlooking the old city, the building was designed to blend in well with the stately embassy buildings that are situated along Sixteenth Street. The apartments of 1661 Crescent Place range in size from having one bedroom with one bath to having three bedrooms with three baths. This comfortable Georgian Revival building was initially home to many upper-level State Department personnel and military officers. Additionally, over the years, a number of members of Congress have lived here, including Senator Claude Pepper of Florida and Senator Thomas Gore of Oklahoma.

Today, the co-op retains a cultured urbane feel with many amenities, such as a roof deck that overlooks Meridian Hill Park and has a broad view of the city to the south. Through the years, many of the apartments have been improved but with a careful attention to retaining the building's original details.

**Joseph A. Younger** (1894–1932) was a native Washingtonian who graduated from the architecture school at George Washington University. After working for a short time at local architecture firms, in 1922, he went into practice for himself. He is remembered for his balanced and graceful buildings. After planning the design of 1661 Crescent Place, Northwest, he went on to design his masterpiece, the truly stunning Kennedy-Warren Apartment Building. The Kennedy-Warren is considered to be the most important privately owned Art Deco building in the nation's capital. As described earlier, the exterior of the building is remarkable for its attention to detail, from its carved limestone eagles that embellish the front entrance to the geometric aluminum spandrels that are flanked by a saw tooth pattern of multicolored brick. However, the Great Depression halted the building's construction, and in 1932, the two developers, Edgar Kennedy and Monroe Warren, were forced to declare bankruptcy. As it became clear to Younger that his wonderful design would not be completed as he had planned, he apparently became depressed, and in May 1932, he committed suicide at his home in the Tilden Gardens Apartment Complex.

## 2540 MASSACHUSETTS AVENUE, NORTHWEST

This imposing and stately building in the Kalorama Heights area was initially known as the Army and Navy. Today, it is simply known by its address. It was planned by architect Harry L. Edwards in 1925 and now has thirty-five apartments. According to James M. Goode's *Best Addresses*, when it opened in 1926, this apartment house was considered to be the finest cooperative in Washington, D.C. Goode wrote, "Its success spurred the development of ever-larger and grander co-ops until the Depression halted all new luxury apartment construction in 1932." A solid brick and stone structure (which originally had twenty-eight apartments), it was designed to have a façade in a dignified English Georgian style.

The stylish entrance to 2540 Massachusetts Avenue, in the Kalorama Heights neighborhood in the northwest. *Photograph by the author.*

Of interesting note, the idea for this building was initially conceived and put together by seventeen military officers who then contacted the Warren brothers and Edmund J. Flynn with their specific proposal for the cooperative. They succeeded well. For many years, the building was primarily a home for military officers, but today, the co-op has members from a variety of professions in our society.

**Harry L. Edwards** (1902–1958) was born in Florida and grew up in Washington, D.C. He graduated from McKinley Technical High School in 1921 and studied architecture at George Washington University's evening school. After apprenticing with several local architects, Edwards entered private practice in 1925. The first District building permit his name appears on as architect was for the Army and Navy Apartment Building, a Georgian Revival–style building that was certainly a superlative first building for an architect. Edwards also worked on planning single-family structures. In a 1927 marketing promotion for the *Washington Star* newspaper,

Edwards designed a model home, which the Warrens then built at the corner of Leland and Elm Streets in Chevy Chase, Maryland. Monroe Warren also employed Edwards to work on the design of the Tilden Gardens project as an associate with the complex's principal landscape architects.

In 1935, Edwards joined the Cafritz Construction Company and designed many buildings for that active firm. After World War II, Edwards left Cafritz to join Alvin L. Aubinoe and Edgar Carroll Beery Jr., and he practiced at Aubinoe, Edwards and Beery until his death in 1958.

## TILDEN GARDENS

The next project the Warren Brothers undertook was the outstanding Tilden Gardens Apartment Complex on Connecticut Avenue, Northwest, which is notable for the skillful siting of its cluster of buildings. The Cleveland Park Apartments project had been a predecessor of the more elaborate garden-style apartment buildings that were soon to develop as the city evolved. Tilden Gardens constructively furthered the basic concept of making the landscape an integral component of a development. This apartment

CENTRAL BUILDING OF TILDEN GARDENS

Tilden Gardens in a presentation drawing from the project architects. The drawing was created for the Warren Brothers. *Courtesy of the Martin Luther King Jr. Memorial Library, D.C. Public Library, Washingtoniana Collection.*

complex of low-rise buildings was planned and laid out on five acres, and it brought together some talented individuals. It was designed primarily by the landscape architectural firm of Parks & Baxter. The triangular-shaped plot of land is bounded by Tilden Street, Sedgwick Street and Connecticut Avenue, and it comprises three X-shaped and three double-X-shaped apartment buildings. The land was purchased by the Warren Brothers from the Chevy Chase Land Company, which, several decades earlier, had acquired an enormous amount of land going to the north. This company then laid out and constructed Connecticut Avenue through the then-rural Northwest Washington, D.C., and up to Chevy Chase, Maryland.

Parks & Baxter worked with architect Harry L. Edwards (familiar to the Warrens), and together, they planned the design and the details of the six Tudor Revival–style buildings. Constructed between 1927 and 1930, the complex was planned as a unified visual whole, and it was designed to include 210 homes. However, as it was being built, the Great Depression descended with a fury, affecting all real estate development in the District, including housing and cooperatives. The project was completed, but with some difficulty.

**Parks & Baxter**. Harvey Paul Baxter (1892–1964) was born in Petersburg, Virginia, and worked for several architectural firms until he was employed by the navy's Bureau of Yards and Docks. He began his own practice in 1922 in partnership with Granville H. Parks (1864–1950), a longtime architect for the Department of Agriculture. Baxter's association with Parks may have come through Parks's brother, Rear Admiral Charles W. Parks, who was chief of the Bureau of Yards and Docks at the time that Baxter worked there. Granville Parks was a D.C. architect who had worked for several city architecture firms before joining the Department of Agriculture. Their firm, Parks & Baxter, apparently produced little in the first several years of its existence, but in 1927, their practice, along with Harry L. Edwards as associate architect, began working on Tilden Gardens. At around the same, their firm also worked on the newly planned Hampshire Gardens Complex. After completing this work, the firm was dissolved in 1930.

For several years, Harvey Baxter continued working for Monroe Warren on other residential projects until World War

II intervened. After the war, Baxter worked for a variety of developers, including Warren, on a wide range of residential projects, both modest and upscale, throughout the greater D.C. area. Separately, Granville Parks returned to work within the Department of Agriculture.

For Tilden Garden, the Warrens had planned a comprehensive project that was set to include a swimming pool and other common amenities, but because of the Great Depression, not everything they planned was built. The first two buildings were completed as two separate co-ops, and the apartments were sold just before the economic crisis took hold. They became 3016 Tilden Street and 3020 Tilden Street, Northwest. But the sales of the next four buildings essentially came to a halt. The construction of these remaining four structures was completed as the economy worsened, and out of necessity, they became, for several years, rental properties. In 1939, the four buildings were combined, organizationally, into one co-op, and the apartments were sold, forming the present-day Tilden Gardens

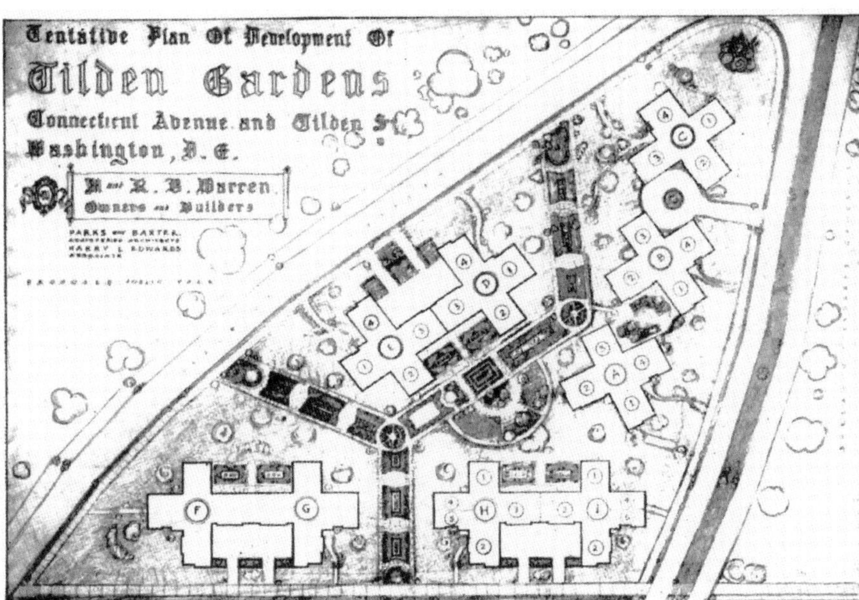


An original site plan of Tilden Gardens, which is located at Connecticut Avenue and Tilden Street. From the *Latch Key*, a co-op magazine produced by the Warren Brothers. *Courtesy of the Tilden Gardens Cooperative.*

Inc. Each of its buildings now elects a representative to the cooperative's board of directors.

According to historian James Goode, Tilden Gardens was the city's most innovative large apartment complex constructed in the 1920s. He wrote, "It was noted not only for its unique landscaping plan but also as the city's largest luxury apartment house built as a co-op—until the Watergate was constructed in the 1960s." Tilden Gardens still remains the grandest of the garden apartment complexes in the District of Columbia. Today, Tilden Gardens has the three independent co-ops and a total of 211 attractive apartments on its mature grounds.

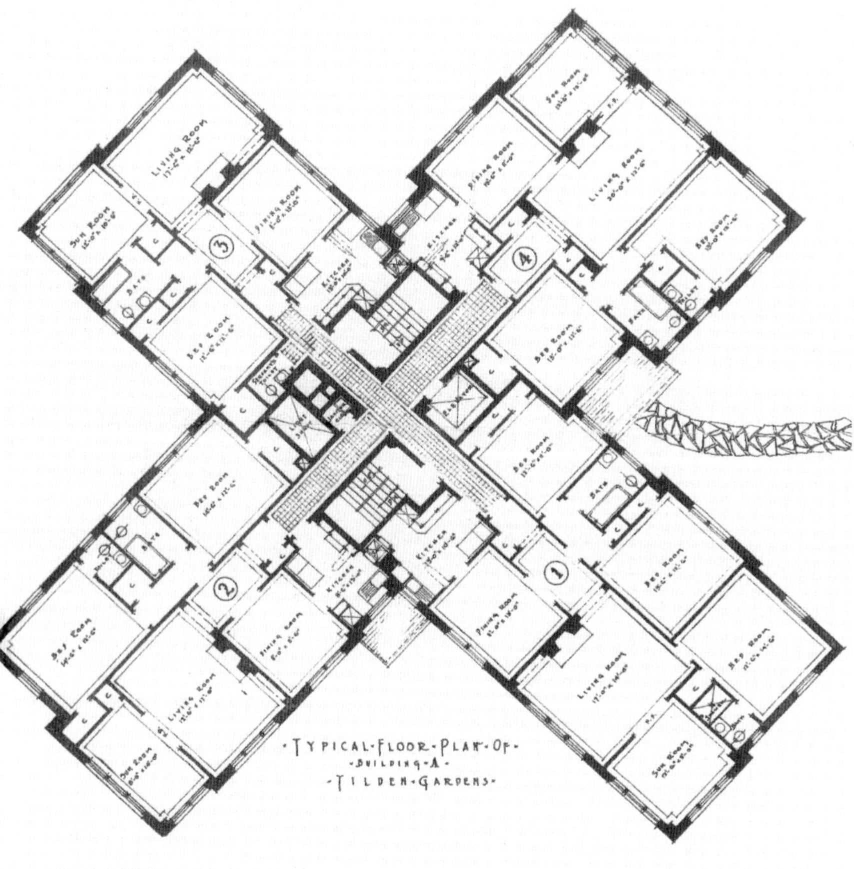


A floor of Building A at Tilden Gardens, showing the skillful layout of the apartment homes. *Courtesy of the Martin Luther King Jr. Memorial Library, D.C. Public Library, Washingtoniana Collection.*

The Tilden Gardens complex and the surrounding area, as seen from the air several years after its completion. The photograph was taken in 1938. *Courtesy of the Historical Society of Washington, D.C.*

As the co-op's website notes about its homes: "Constructed of red brick and trimmed with Indiana limestone, the Tudor Revival buildings are set among charming terraced gardens. The spacious apartments were thoughtfully designed with meticulous attention to detail." To further the agreeable appearance of its Tudor Revival style, the buildings were designed with hipped roofs and dormers. Half-timber and stucco surfaces were also used. The Warren Brothers also carefully continued on with their high standards of construction. The parking garages for the buildings were designed to remain unobtrusive on the property. Each apartment featured the quality details seen in the upscale homes of the day; many homes in Tilden Gardens have leaded glass windows and most have enclosed sunrooms.

With an eye on creating something special, the architects studied other similar projects around the country, looking for smart ideas, and thus, the complex was built with good attention to detail and with an obvious sense of energy and enthusiasm. The Warrens even established a newsletter, the *Latch Key*, to highlight and promote co-op activities. Originally, the apartments sold for between $10,600 and $16,165 each, about the cost of a typical single-family home in Cleveland Park at the time.

Today, travelers along Connecticut Avenue can see and appreciate the established trees on the property and the buildings that are comfortably nestled within the co-op's landscaping.

## Hampshire Gardens

The ambitious Hampshire Gardens project is a somewhat less well-known part of the history of housing cooperatives in Washington, D.C., but it is a relatively important one, in part because it is yet another manifestation of just how damaging the Great Depression was to our nation's civic life.

While the Warren Brothers were busy arranging and building Tilden Gardens, Edmund Flynn was busy with his own plans for a truly grand real estate development to be placed in the city's Petworth neighborhood, about two miles east of Tilden Gardens. The proposal called for Hampshire Gardens to be located near what was then known as the Old Soldiers Home. (It is now called the Armed Forces Retirement Home.)

As described in the co-op's National Register of Historic Places registration form (prepared by the National Park Service) when the project received its historic designation in 1994:

> *The Hampshire Garden Apartment Buildings was one of the earliest garden apartment developments in the city. At the time, it was conceived to be the largest. The original plan occupied 50 acres between Rock Creek Park and the Soldier's Home. It covered 25 city blocks and was designed to have 2,500 apartments with the capacity of housing 7,500 people. The location of Hampshire Gardens in "near wilderness" was a bold step for the developers. They believed that a well-planned community in verdant surroundings was an irresistible combination and certainly outweighed the distant location; the developers recognized that the newly extended streetcar lines made the property accessible.*

However, the National Register further noted:

> *Hampered by the city's economic instability during the Depression, the developers were compelled to curb their grandiose scheme. Consequently, they completed one city block of the original plan.*

That block, which is located on New Hampshire Avenue at Farragut Street, Northwest, contains nine buildings with a total of 102 apartments that are arranged within the block's five acres. Today, it continues to operate

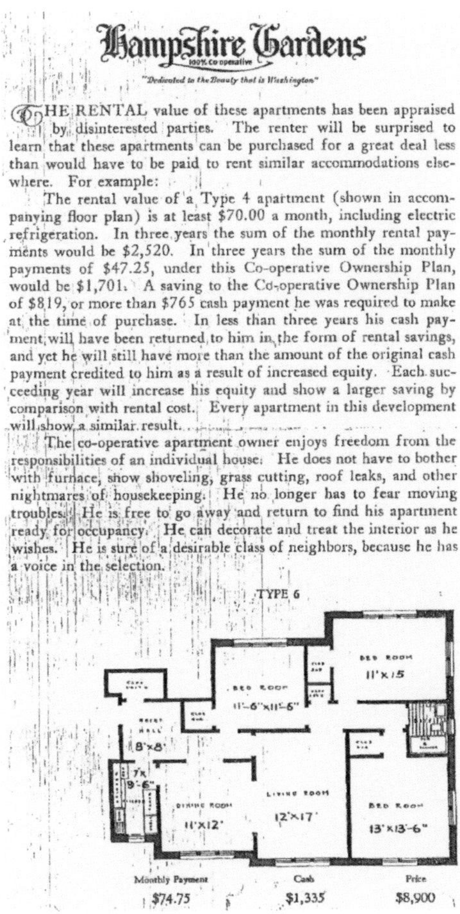

**Hampshire Gardens**

100% Co-operative

"Dedicated to the Beauty that is Washington"

THE RENTAL value of these apartments has been appraised by disinterested parties. The renter will be surprised to learn that these apartments can be purchased for a great deal less than would have to be paid to rent similar accommodations elsewhere. For example:

The rental value of a Type 4 apartment (shown in accompanying floor plan) is at least $70.00 a month, including electric refrigeration. In three years the sum of the monthly rental payments would be $2,520. In three years the sum of the monthly payments of $47.25, under this Co-operative Ownership Plan, would be $1,701. A saving to the Co-operative Ownership Plan of $819, or more than $765 cash payment he was required to make at the time of purchase. In less than three years his cash payment will have been returned to him in the form of rental savings, and yet he will still have more than the amount of the original cash payment credited to him as a result of increased equity. Each succeeding year will increase his equity and show a larger saving by comparison with rental cost. Every apartment in this development will show a similar result.

The co-operative apartment owner enjoys freedom from the responsibilities of an individual house. He does not have to bother with furnace, snow shoveling, grass cutting, roof leaks, and other nightmares of housekeeping. He no longer has to fear moving troubles. He is free to go away and return to find his apartment ready for occupancy. He can decorate and treat the interior as he wishes. He is sure of a desirable class of neighbors, because he has a voice in the selection.

TYPE 6



| Monthly Payment | Cash | Price |
|---|---|---|
| $74.75 | $1,335 | $8,900 |

A part of the sales brochure for the Hampshire Gardens Project. The sales price of the apartment, with the floor plan shown, was $8,900—not cheap for 1929 but well worth the money. *Courtesy of the Edmund J. Flynn Company.*

as a cooperative and is an attractive element in its neighborhood, a smaller piece of the large dream that Edmund J. Flynn had planned. That dream was to create a solid and visually pleasant community and to provide homes for the stable and dependable middle-class residents of Washington, D.C. The apartments were comparable to the nearby houses—not grand and showy, but they were good-looking, sturdy and practical.

Flynn had set up the Hampshire Gardens Development Corporation Inc. to be the formal developer of the project. Working with builder Joseph Shapiro, Flynn planned the details, and together, they started the actual work. Shapiro was a noted Washington, D.C. builder who had constructed private residences and apartment buildings in the city during the early decades of the twentieth century; in the mid-1920s, he had worked closely with George T. Santmyers on residences in Woodley Park.

**George T. Santmyers** (1889–1960) Santmyers moved to Washington as a teenager and studied architecture in the city at the Washington Architecture Club Atelier before apprenticing in local architecture firms. He opened his own firm in 1909 and continued his practice for almost fifty years. As he progressed, he became one of the city's most prolific and important architects of the twentieth century. While Santmyers is credited with designing a variety of commercial buildings, banks, churches, public garages and thousands of single-family residences, he is most celebrated for his contribution to apartment building architecture, and he worked in most areas of the nation's capital. As the architect of over 440 apartment buildings in the course of his long career, Santmyers devoted his skills and energy to producing attractively designed buildings with pragmatic plans. Most of his work was for the city's commercial property developers designing speculative structures. His ability to craft distinctive creations within a variety of budgets gave the city a fine legacy of buildings. When he was given a larger budget, his creative designs excelled.

His work included a range of styles, from Tudor Revival to Gothic to Colonial Revival, and as the Art Deco style became popular, he created some memorable apartment buildings in that motif. Two of the more prominent buildings he designed are 3901 Connecticut Avenue, Northwest (1927), and 2101 Connecticut Avenue, Northwest (1929). A large number of his other works were typical residential structures, usually brick; many were row houses. Today, numerous and diverse pieces of the basic background landscape of the city are composed of buildings designed by George T. Santmyers. He worked right until his death in 1960.

Flynn and Shapiro had high hopes for the new project. The construction permits for each of the nine buildings list James E. Cooper and George T. Santmyers as the architects (with Santmyers working primarily on the interiors), along with Parks and Baxter, who were to be responsible for the landscape design as associate architects.

Again, an excerpt from the Park Service's National Register of Historic Places registration form:

> *The two-story buildings are located in Square 3324 and bounded by Emerson, Farragut, and 3rd Streets, and New Hampshire Avenue, N.W. The individual buildings are skilled interpretations of the Tudor Revival style and are sited around a landscaped courtyard and amidst gardens. The gardens provide a verdant setting, while the small-scale Tudor Revival buildings invoke images of a bucolic English village. The exterior details were of the highest caliber in middle-class apartment buildings. The exteriors remain true to the architect's 1929 design. The landscaped gardens have also remained intact.*
>
> *Hampshire Gardens offered beautifully landscaped gardens, architecturally pleasing exterior designs, quality materials, well-planned interiors, and notable features such as solariums, built-in tubs and showers, tiled bathrooms, and custom kitchen cabinets.*

Initially, the co-op units sold well, even though some in the city's real estate world had labeled the project "Flynn's Folly." The finished complex, although it covered just one square city block, had some nice amenities, such as a gym, which was unusual at the time. Its residents also developed a strong community spirit. But the dramatic change in the national economy also changed the project's plans. From a June 1982 article in the *Washington Post*:

> *After opening, the 102-unit Hampshire Gardens attracted the...federal workers who were the target of the builders' advertising, recalled Edmund C. Flynn, son of one of the developers, Edmund J. Flynn, and now president of the District real estate firm that bears his father's name. The Flynn family lived in Hampshire Gardens from 1929 to 1948.*
>
> *The nine two-story buildings were to be the first phase of the cooperative's development, but the stock market crashed in 1929 and the Depression ended those expansion plans, Flynn said.*
>
> *Hampshire Gardens formally opened about two months before the stocks tumbled, but the cooperative weathered the Depression with little problem, he said. Some residents fell behind in their shareholder payments, but rather than foreclose, the co-op had them move out and rented the units for them, he said. Once the owners were financially back on their feet, they were allowed to return, Flynn said.*

After the one square block of Hampshire Gardens was completed, the other adjacent and undeveloped city blocks that were planned to be included in the complex sat vacant for a time, but in the later 1930s, they were taken up and built on as the federal government grew and the Great Depression

A modern view of an entrance at the Hampshire Gardens Apartment Complex, which is located at New Hampshire Avenue and Farragut Street, Northwest. *Photograph by the author.*

eased. These new construction projects were mainly well-constructed row houses as well as some small apartment houses. The Tudor Revival style was used in several areas of this new construction; this was likely done to emulate the appearance of the well-regarded buildings of Hampshire Gardens. Indeed, with its many thoughtful details, Hampshire Gardens was used as the model for a number of subsequent garden apartment complexes that were built in the area, such as Colonial Village in Arlington, Virginia, and some of the New Deal housing projects, such as the Falkland Apartments in Silver Spring in suburban Maryland.

BY THE MID-1920S, THE cooperative model, as seen in Washington, D.C., had grown in popularity and public notice. Thus, a few other local developers also toyed with the idea and decided to build co-op apartment houses. Many of the buildings were designed in the English Tudor or Colonial Revival styles, which mimicked the look of many of the nicer single-family homes that were being built at the time.

## THE CLYDESDALE

One of Washington, D.C.'s other developers was the prolific Harry Wardman. He dove into the new co-op market with a stylish new apartment building named the Clydesdale. Wardman had evidently noted how three of his recently

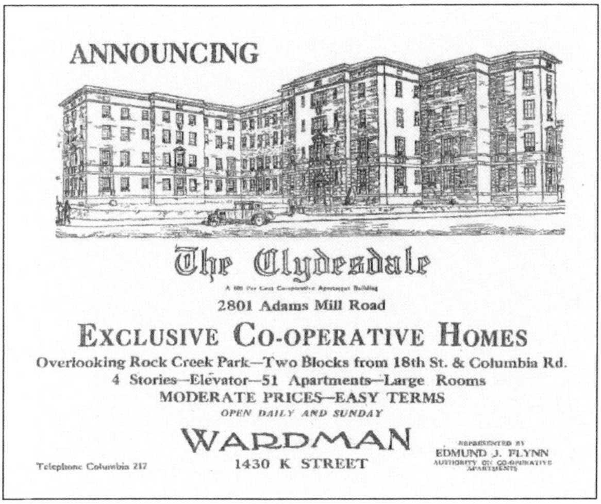


2800 Adams Mill Road in Northwest. A newspaper advertisement from Harry Wardman, dated April 11, 1926. *Courtesy of the* Washington Post.

constructed buildings were sold in the first group of co-op conversions, and he decided to build a few new buildings as co-ops. The Clydesdale, located at 2800 Adams Mill Road in Lanier Heights, was completed in 1926, just as Wardman was also developing his famous Wardman Park Hotel. The fifty-two-unit apartment building shares some of the same architectural details as the hotel. The Clydesdale was successfully marketed as a Flynn co-op. Today, the cooperative continues to be a prominent and attractive presence in its neighborhood near the National Zoo.

## NEW YORK AVENUE, NORTHWEST

A large downtown development of cooperative apartment homes was also built by Harry Wardman in 1926. At around the same time as the start of the Clydesdale in 1925, Wardman began constructing a group of five apartment buildings, which he erected along New York Avenue at First and M Streets, Northwest, just west of North Capitol Street. The newspaper advertisements for this new project stated, "The largest Development of Co-operative Apartments South of New York City. Five Magnificent Buildings....Edmund J. Flynn (Authority in Co-operative Apartments) Representing Wardman Construction Company."

This group of solidly built, four-story brick-and-stone structures were designed in the English Georgian style by architect Eugene Waggaman and contained a total of 145 apartments. The buildings sat close to the

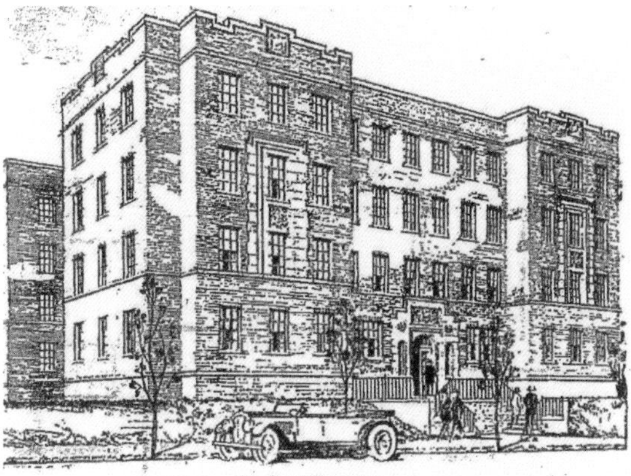

A contemporary advertisement for Wardman's downtown apartment home development. The building shown here was located at 55 M Street, Northwest. *Courtesy of the Edmund J. Flynn Company.*

downtown area of Washington, D.C., not far from Union Station. The apartments were prominently marketed by the Flynn Company to the growing middle class. But in a brief number of years, as the downtown area became, at first, too urban (and, in fact, quite a bit industrial) and then deteriorated, these cooperative apartments grew increasingly less attractive to home buyers. Between 1946 and 1960, the buildings were sold separately to outside investors and became rental properties. Four of these structures still remain as sturdy city housing. In the 1970s, these properties were successfully converted into condominiums.

## THE DEVELOPER: HARRY WARDMAN

Harry Wardman (1872–1938) was born in England and came to Washington, D.C., in 1902 to work in building construction. Through both diligence and the expertise he acquired, he later became known as *the* Washington real estate developer of the early twentieth century. His buildings included landmark hotels, luxury apartment buildings and a great many row houses. At the time of his death on March 18, 1938, it was estimated that about one-tenth of the residents of Washington, D.C., were living in homes built by Harry Wardman.

As the most prolific residential developer in Washington, D.C.'s history, Wardman continues to be justly famous. In most of his projects, he served as both the developer and builder, and in many instances, he would sell a project after its completion. This allowed him to effectively create a funding stream that provided him with the financing to arrange an ongoing building-

Harry Wardman, a renowned developer and builder of many homes in the neighborhoods of Washington, D.C. *Courtesy of the Library of Congress.*

development system. He became quite wealthy but lost most of his assets in the Great Depression. Nevertheless, he continued on with his firm, crafting residential buildings until he died. He is especially noted for building the Hay-Adams Hotel near the White House, the distinguished British Embassy and the Warden Park Hotel. In all, he constructed around four hundred apartment buildings.

Although Wardman built just a few cooperatives in the District, his influence on many of the city's neighborhoods where co-ops are prevalent was very large. The design and scale of his developments often set the tone for broad portions of some residential areas.

In a separate project, another local developer, Charles Hunt, constructed the well-made five-story brick building at 2707 Adams Mill Road, Northwest, in Lanier Heights. Designed by the prolific George T. Santmyers in an appealing transitional English Domestic Art Deco style, it was completed in 1927 and opened as a cooperative. It has fifty apartments.

Separately, the Porter, located at 3600 Connecticut Avenue, Northwest, was completed in 1927 by the Cafritz Construction Company. While its construction was in progress, Morris Cafritz decided that the property would be developed as a co-op and arranged for the necessary marketing. This four-story brick building is across the street from the larger Broadmoor Apartments in Cleveland Park. The Porter is a Spanish-style structure with twenty-eight units arranged in seven vertical tiers, with seven units per floor. The architect was the noted Harvey H. Warwick.

**Connecticut Courts Cooperative**, located in the District's Chevy Chase neighborhood, at 5112 Connecticut Avenue, Northwest, was built as a cooperative by developer Harry Brannow in 1927. This attractive three-story Beaux-Arts–style building with pleasant porches has thirty-five apartments. It was designed by local architects Doleman and McCaw.

DURING THESE YEARS, THE co-op movement continued to attract attention across the country. It was a time of robust urban growth in many areas, and large numbers of people wanted to establish their own homes. Other cities took notice of the co-op movement as it took hold in New York, Washington, D.C., and Chicago, and in some of these other cities, home builders went about creating similar developments.

But throughout the twentieth century, the rare situation of a careless co-op creation would at times occur, mainly in smaller buildings. In these cases, a co-op would be started, typically with good intentions, but would be organized without proper forethought, leading to its collapse as a viable co-op. There were also a very few unusual experiments (often among friends) that did not succeed, and there were very rare situations in which a project was little more than a developer's get-rich-quick scheme.

## A PROBLEM ARISES

As co-ops attracted more attention, that tiny number of inexperienced—or even shady—developers did observe the idea's rising popularity, and their activity in the new world of co-ops caused some trouble. And so, following complaints from a few D.C. citizens, Congress took notice and held a hearing on the subject. A *Washington Star* article published on January 17, 1929, titled "Apartment Probe Starts Tomorrow: Inquiry Into Co-operative Projects" reported, "When informed of the plans for the inquiry, R. Bates Warren… stated that he welcomed the move, which he held would likely demonstrate publicly the difference between good and bad projects."

The article noted that the complaints given to Congress reported that the Parkway Co-op on Connecticut Avenue had failed financially, with most of its co-op members losing money. The Parkway Apartments had been envisioned as an eighty-three-unit structure designed by architect F. Russell White. The building was started in 1927 and completed later in 1928. But the developer, Arthur M. Suit, had failed to sell enough units and defaulted on the construction loans in mid-1928, and he quickly left town. The individuals, the prospective co-op apartment purchasers, then lost their down payments when the building was sold. The Parkway, when finally finished, was opened as a rental property.

From the article: "Mr. Warren pointed out that this building was the only one of more than 40 co-operative projects in Washington to fail with any loss to purchasers of stock." The hearing was concluded with the co-op concept, overall, being exonerated. In the end, even though this was an isolated case, Congress did enact legislation that protected co-op associations and their members from improper developer use of funds while construction was still underway. At the time, well-planned co-ops weathered this hit of bad press surrounding an instance of bad execution, and the overall concept continued to successfully move forward.

WHAT THE WARREN FAMILY, along with Edmund Flynn, Harry Wardman and the others, did as home builders was important for the city. They developed structures that had practical, useful designs and were solidly well-constructed buildings. Generally, their buildings set good examples for other, later developers—with notably thoughtful civic placements of their buildings. This creation of high-quality multiunit structures helped to not only house city residents but also allowed the city to grow in a forward-looking manner. In addition, some of these buildings were built to appeal to a variety of the wealthier people who brought a certain cachet to their neighborhoods and, thus, often helped define the character of them. The best of the Warren buildings established the standards for a few sumptuous luxury apartment buildings that were soon to be built in the later 1920s. But in addition, they also created a number of properties that were within reach of many middle-class and upper-middle-class residents.

Home ownership and stable communities with residents who have personal interest in the health of their city are definitely good things. Clearly, co-ops have helped build such communities in Washington, D.C.

# 3

# 1941–1959: WORLD WAR II AND GROWTH AFTER THE WAR

With the disruption of war coming to the United States in 1941, Washington was dramatically affected in a great many ways. For one thing, there was an immediate need for a large number of additional multiunit buildings in Washington, D.C., as people swarmed into the city to help with the administrative tasks connected with the war. Some prominent rental buildings were also built at this time. In general, though, most new residents simply managed to squeeze into the city.

During the Great Depression, there had been little growth of new co-op housing in Washington, D.C. Nevertheless, throughout the 1930s and into the 1940s, the existing cooperative apartment buildings in the District generally continued on, with almost all of them doing well or at least managing to stay healthy during the lingering years of the Great Depression. Plus, the federal government had expanded. By 1940, the co-ops that had been left organizationally unfinished as associations had almost all been sold to co-op share owners. Cooperatives, overall, continued to mature and settle into the city, but a few of these properties—those without a sound financial footing—did disband and fade into history. Those few were either sold and returned to operating as rental properties or were purchased and redeveloped. Thus, the sturdy co-ops, the ones that we still see thriving today, continued to provide good homes to many residents of the District and were good financial investments for their families.

After the war, a number of dynamic housing changes took hold and developed throughout the United States. During this time, the manner in which Americans viewed their cities and how they wanted to individually use the nation's urban areas shifted. The concept of a happy suburban life, with each family being in their own "mini-estate," blossomed. At this time, civic writings boosting suburbia were major factors in this shift, as were some major real estate developers. The federal government also played a significant role in this shift, which led to declining populations in cities. World War II veterans received housing subsidies, primarily for new homes in new areas. This was coupled with the development of brand-new road systems, which made suburban living more attractive and had the additional national growth benefit of many more sales of new cars. The suburbs of Washington, D.C., greatly expanded, but many people still enjoyed city living.

In the District, some of the better apartment houses that were still rental buildings—particularly those that had not had their units broken up during the Great Depression or during the war—became more desirable to city dwellers. Many of these were converted into cooperatives during the late 1940s and early 1950s. This group of buildings included some of the District's most well-known present-day cooperatives, such as the Ontario, the Broadmoor and the Westchester.

There are several reasons why these postwar conversions moved forward and succeeded, and there were a number of methods used to create them. In some cases, the buildings were put up for sale by their original developers and owners. In other cases, the building's residents saw that forming a co-op was a good way to secure their continued ability to stay in their homes and gain home equity. Some investment companies saw a business opportunity in creating conversions. For whatever the reason, in most of these situations, the Edmund J. Flynn Company was involved and was actively helping move the process along by providing smart marketing strategies, working to organize some of the projects (financially and operationally) and conducting the sales transactions for the apartments.

In some neighborhoods, the technical ending of racial segregation in the early 1950s—even though segregation's abolition was certainly appropriate and necessary—had an adverse effect on some residential areas as white flight took hold, with many white residents choosing to abruptly leave for the suburbs. However, others stayed and helped the city move ahead. Consequently, this state of affairs had an influence on several of the building conversions that were then going forward. Without a doubt, a great many members of D.C.'s co-op community looked toward a better, integrated future for the city, with most of them certainly looking at their purchases as smart decisions. For a short time, others saw conversion as a way to control membership, but integration progressively came to all areas. In any case, these transitions from rental to co-op ownership helped support and stabilize neighborhoods. These new conversions also certainly resulted in the continued existence of some fine apartment house structures in the District. Then, as now, a large number of cooperatives sat as attractive anchor buildings in their neighborhoods.

Starting in 1920, many of the early co-ops had some restrictions on membership in their associations as well as local covenants and other forms of social control. These restrictions typically mirrored the community standards and behaviors of their day, standards that can be somewhat surprising to learn about today, given the changes in common attitudes since the early twentieth century. Some of the controls were simple, such as not permitting children to live in the co-op; often such regulations were lifted or modified as the co-op grew and the shared wishes of the owners changed. Over time, the house rules of most buildings have evolved, and today, co-ops and most condos all use similar sets of modern guidelines.

Other early restrictions were stricter and more inflexible and were sometimes ethically harmful and, in today's world, downright repugnant. Covenants were used to exclude members on the basis of race and religion. Sometimes, covenants weren't necessary, as the restrictive actions could be achieved with unspoken behavior. Such unspoken actions were effectively used throughout society for years to wrongly discriminate. Over the past fifty years, these biased restrictions have been principally eliminated for good.

But today, cooperatives employ a number of rules that they apply properly and evenly. These rules govern financial matters and manage the use of apartments and other activities, allowing co-ops to function reasonably and responsibly and make decisions for the benefit of the group as a whole as well as for individual members.

## THE HAWARDEN

The Hawarden, located at 1419 R Street, Northwest, became a co-op in 1949, due in large part to an emerging Black middle class that had an interest in urban home ownership, and it was aided by the growing acceptance of African Americans in the mainstream society of the nation. A good measure of this shift occurred because World War II had shown everyone that all citizens of the nation could work and live together. These steps toward

The Hawarden, built in 1902, was an early example of the modern apartment building in the District at 1419 R Street, Northwest. *Photograph by the author.*

acceptance and home ownership led to the official—if not accepted by all—desegregation of the 1950s. As the city of Washington, D.C., like the nation, slowly moved toward the better treatment of African Americans, more housing opportunities became available to them. These opportunities came about because additional neighborhoods were opened up to African Americans, partially because of white flight and the growing availability of better-paying jobs.

The Hawarden is a solid five-story Romanesque Revival brick building. Designed by George S. Cooper, it was completed in 1902 and originally had twenty units. The Hawarden and its matching next-door building, the Gladstone, were the first twin apartment buildings constructed in the city, and they were among the first apartment buildings in D.C. that were designed specifically for white middle-class citizens. Not that long after their construction, the neighborhood around the buildings, which was situated near the U Street corridor, famously became a predominantly African American area. When the Hawarden became a co-op, it had no racial restrictions on co-op membership. The Gladstone continued operating as a rental for several more decades until it was converted into a condominium. Both buildings were added to the National Register of Historic Places in 1994.

## The Broadmoor

The Broadmoor is among Washington, D.C.'s more prominent and admired cooperatives. Known for its attractive architectural styling, expansive landscaping, excellent building amenities and list of distinguished residents, the property was built between 1927 and 1929. It was one of the first luxury rental apartment buildings to be built along Connecticut Avenue north of the zoo, and it remains among the most distinguished residences in the nation's capital today. It has been a cooperative since 1948, when it was converted by the Flynn Company. (The apartments sold quickly.)

The first residents of the Broadmoor were moving in just as the stock market collapsed in the fall of 1929, but the building carried on. An early rental brochure described the property—which, at the time, was thought to be agreeably far out of town—as "the home of prominent business executives, senators, representatives, army and navy officers and of a select cross-section of official Washington." Most of the apartments were available on long-term leases, but other units were offered as hotel suites to guests and were rented out by the day or week. The public facilities, most notably the dining room—which, prior to 1938, was known as the Silver Grill—became a popular site for wedding receptions, school proms and other social functions. At the time, the amenities included a beauty shop, a barbershop, a pastry shop, a valet and laundry service and a newsstand. Most of these are now long-closed features, but the co-op continues to provide a pleasant lower-

The Broadmoor Cooperative, from the mid-1950s, showing its expansive grounds and attractive building. The wings of the structure add to its good visual appearance. *Courtesy of the Edmund J. Flynn Company.*

level library and a spacious community and party room. The building also possesses what is considered to be one of the city's first underground garages located under an apartment building.

The large structure, which was built by Washington, D.C. developers Harry Bralove and Edward C. Ernst, was designed by architect Joseph H. Abel, who later crafted many other well-regarded apartment buildings in Washington, D.C. With the Broadmoor, Abel, at the young age of twenty-two, was allowed to shine. On this expansive property, the structure was designed to be a seen as a standalone presence. It was built on vacant land that had a rear hill sloping east into the woods of Rock Creek Park.

The dramatic U-shaped building is set back from its brick entrance gateposts. The driveway up to the entrance also has a brick sidewalk that was laid in a herringbone pattern next to a distinctive curvilinear brick wall. The building features projecting towers and bays with a brick porte-cochère entrance. The façades are textured with rough bricks that project from the surface in random patterns. The featured elements are made of Indiana limestone and include hand-carved heraldic tower accents and balconies with limestone cross motifs. (Some of this information is courtesy of the Broadmoor Cooperative website.)

**Joseph H. Abel** (1905–1985) was born in Washington, D.C., and graduated from the city's Central High School. He began his architectural career as a draftsman for George T. Santmyers. Abel then enrolled at the George Washington University while still working on other projects. After graduating in 1932, he briefly worked for Arthur Heaton. Later in 1932, he joined the practice of architect Charles E. Dillon. The firm of Dillon & Abel was the first to introduce the International style to Washington, D.C. In the late 1930s, several of the firm's designs, such as 2929 Connecticut Avenue, were notable examples of that style. Dillon & Abel designed numerous residences throughout the city but gained recognition for their trademark light tan brick apartment houses that featured ribbon windows, unadorned façades and glass block detailing around their entrances. But Abel was adept with other styles, as can be seen at the Broadmoor, and he was also skilled at effectively laying out the wings of larger apartment buildings. Over time, he was a principal in several local architectural firms.

Additionally, Joseph Abel wrote several well-known books on architecture, explaining and promoting the design and construction of midcentury American apartment buildings. He especially pointed out the need for good interior planning for modern people. Abel died at the age of eighty in 1985.

Over the years, the Broadmoor has been home to a wide range of prominent Washington, D.C. residents. This has included some major political figures, including the outspoken senator Huey Long of Louisiana. For a brief time, Richard Nixon was also a resident. The building was once home to many members of the Washington Senators baseball team. For several years, labor leader George Meany lived here.

A modern view of the stylish porte-cochère entrance of the Broadmoor Cooperative. *Courtesy of the Library of Congress, the Carol M. Highsmith Archive.*

OF INTEREST TO CO-OPS in D.C. was the notable legal ruling that had its beginning at the Broadmoor. This involved a significant court case in 1996, which was initiated by the co-op and helped all co-ops in the District retain control of how apartments in co-ops can be used by residents. The resolution of this basic question has helped permit co-ops to set internal rules on issues such as subletting. This has allowed co-ops to remain primarily owner-occupied properties. As noted elsewhere, this use rule can definitely help define the character of a multiunit building.

Specifically, the Broadmoor played a key role in resolving the question of whether cooperatives in D.C. can impose surcharges on co-op members who rent out their units. In the case of *Kelley v. Broadmoor Cooperative Apartments* (1996), the D.C. Court of Appeals, in reviewing a challenge brought by a Broadmoor member, upheld the authority of co-ops to impose rental surcharges.

# NAYLOR GARDENS

By 1948, a growing number of residential buildings had emerged as candidates for conversion into city cooperatives. The large Naylor Gardens Complex was one such conversion. During World War II, the federal government planned and built several apartment communities in the D.C. area for people who had come to town to help with the war effort. Naylor Gardens was one of these communities.

The Defense Homes Corporation, a federal wartime agency, laid out Naylor Gardens in 1942. This garden apartment complex, which was built in much the same manner as the more well-known McLean Gardens, is near the Suitland Parkway in southeast Washington, D.C. It shares the same attractive design and style as the McLean Gardens property. Both complexes were very solidly built. Naylor Gardens opened in February 1943 and was converted into a co-op in 1948. After the war, in 1946, the federal government decided to divest itself of its recently built housing developments. At Naylor Gardens, they formed the Veterans Cooperative Housing Association and then worked out the necessary planning for the conversion.

Situated on a forty-three-acre campus, the co-op has handsome brick buildings with landscaped grounds. Naylor Gardens is very attractively laid

A view of Naylor Gardens in 1949, on Erie Street in Southwest. *Courtesy of the Historical Society of Washington, D.C., John P. Wymer Photograph Collection.*

out in a park-like setting. The buildings are rich in city heritage and have been hailed by the *Washington Post* as one of D.C.'s best-kept secrets, as they sit in a quiet corner of the District. The cooperative is such a defining part of its neighborhood that the neighborhood itself is now known as Naylor Gardens. Located near the Maryland line, today, it contains 748 good-looking units that provide homes for typically middle-income residents.

The complex offers ten different types of traditional, expansive floor plans, and the apartments have a comfortable feel, with nine-foot ceilings. There are one-, two- and three-bedroom units as well as community rooms and other amenities.

## Meridian Hill Studio

A small thirteen-unit cooperative—but one that deserves to be noted—is Meridian Hill Studio, located at 2633 Fifteenth Street, Northwest, not far from Meridian Hill Park. The building resembles an Arts and Crafts version of a French chateau and retains most of its original detailing. It was designed by George Oakley Totten and opened in 1923 as a rental building. The units were designed for working artists and artistic types and vary greatly in size and shape. Some are three levels high, and several have two-story-tall living rooms. A few of the apartments have large gallery-sized rooms.

Meridian Hill Studio was built by Mary Foote Henderson, who planned the building to be one more part of her overall vision of a cultured, special neighborhood around Sixteenth Street, Northwest. The property was converted to a cooperative in 1941, an early time in the decade (prewar) for such a conversion.

## The Senate Cooperative

Situated on Capitol Hill, just behind the Supreme Court Building, is the Senate Cooperative, a traditional Classical Revival apartment building that was constructed in 1915. The sixteen-unit structure at 115 Second Street, Northeast, is conveniently located for members of Congress, and over the years, it has been home to an assortment of legislators from around the nation. The property was originally developed by S.A. Manuel and was designed by architect George P. Stales. It was converted to co-op ownership in 1947.

## A Continuing Number of Conversions

While the postwar period saw several new co-ops being created in various areas of the city, most of the conversions that occurred after 1945 happened in the northwest quadrant. Several of the conversions included what are considered to be some of the very finest apartment buildings in the D.C. region. A large number of them are included in James Goode's *Best Addresses* apartment house book. A few, such as 2500 Massachusetts Avenue, Northwest (which became a co-op in 1948), are quiet but special properties that only have a small number of apartments each. The following addresses are examples of some of the more well-known buildings that became cooperatives in this era.

### *The Avondale*

The Avondale, located at 1734 P Street, Northwest, is another cooperative located in the city's Dupont Circle neighborhood. Built by Harry Wardman and designed by Frank Russell White, one of Wardman's most-often-utilized architects, it first opened in 1914 as a rental apartment building. The Avondale has an interesting history. As noted earlier, this property was among the first ten already-built structures that was converted into a cooperative in 1920. However, in 1940, the shareholder owners decided to sell the property to an outside investor. Then, in 1949, in a turnabout, the investor, along with the residents, chose to reestablish the property as a cooperative building, and they successfully did so, creating the present-day co-op.

The Avondale contains thirty-nine units that are divided into an approximately equal number of one-bedroom, two-bedroom and three-bedroom units. The front of the building features an impressive iron-and-glass marquee. The Avondale, which is well known in its neighborhood, is noted for the attractive qualities of its apartments—high ceilings, wood floors, fine plasterwork and generously sized rooms.

## *The Altamont*

A view of the Altamont from around 1924 by Theodor Horydczak (1890–1971), a noted photographer of Washington's architecture. *Courtesy of the Library of Congress.*

Atop one of the hills that encircle downtown D.C., at the corner of Wyoming Avenue and Columbia Road, Northwest, is the Altamont, a beautiful and elaborate structure. Sitting in the Kalorama Triangle neighborhood, it was built with twenty-seven apartments and, today, contains fifty-two. The building is exceptional, with many beautiful details, including its distinctive rooftop pavilion. It was converted into a co-op in 1949.

The Altamont is special in a number of ways. According to James Goode in *Best Addresses*, "The Altamont was one of the great luxury apartments of Washington when it opened in 1916. Its history and design remain among the most interesting of any apartment house standing in the city today."

Architect Arthur B. Heaton designed the Altamont in the Mission Revival style, which was popular at the time, and its design included Italianate accents. The details of the building's first-class construction are remarkable. The large public rooms on the first floor off of the spacious entrance area were completed with fine handcrafted stonework. The seven-story Altamont now consists of fifty-two residences of varying sizes, with the apartments retaining period details, including high ceilings, fireplaces and hardwood floors. Some units have been broken up, but the apartments retain spacious rooms as well as modern conveniences, such as walk-in closets, which were unique for their time.

**Arthur B. Heaton** (1875–1951) was a native Washingtonian and graduated from the District's Central High School in 1892. He then apprenticed for a time under Paul Petz, the chief designer of the Library of Congress. After studying in Europe, Heaton opened his own practice in 1898. He was prolific, designing more than one thousand buildings. Many are listed in the National Register of Historic Places. He was very active in the cultural life of Washington and was the first supervising architect of the Washington National Cathedral during the church's initial construction. His various buildings helped establish the mid-city neighborhoods of Cleveland Park, Kalorama Triangle and Woodley Park. Between 1900 and 1940, Heaton designed twenty-eight apartment buildings, including the Highland Apartments (now the Churchill Hotel) at 1914 Connecticut Avenue, Northwest.

The Altamont is one of Heaton's most outstanding apartment designs and is a centerpiece property in the Kalorama Triangle Historic District. Most of the residential buildings he designed were private residences. He provided the plans for hundreds of homes in the Burleith neighborhood. In addition, he designed homes for many of Washington's prominent citizens, including Gilbert H. Grosvenor, the first president of the National Geographic Society. His work was wide-ranging and included two buildings on the campus of George Washington University. On Connecticut Avenue, in Northwest, he designed the Park and Shop, one of the nation's first planned neighborhood shopping centers with off-street parking.

In his personal life, Arthur Heaton was well known for his active civic work and his support of good housing in the city. An advocate for sound and adequate District homes, he participated in efforts to clean up the slums and improve Washington, D.C.'s buildings. He was a leader of a movement to repair and restore houses, which also provided jobs during the Great Depression. In 1940, for the city, Heaton worked on the design of an eighteen-building public housing complex located in Southeast. In 1941, Heaton was named a fellow of the American Institute of Architects. After his death in 1941, his large collection of drawings was donated to the Library of Congress.

When it opened, the Altamont contained twenty-seven apartments: four efficiencies, fourteen one-bedroom units, three two-bedroom units and six four-bedroom units. On the fourth, fifth and sixth floors, there were only three apartments per floor, and each apartment had two working fireplaces. The top of the building provided a splendid place to escape the city streets below, with two summer pavilions on the roof and a dining room on the penthouse level. Also, when the Altamont first opened, the basement contained a billiards room, a barbershop, a beauty parlor, a servants' dining room, a refrigeration room and a laundry room. Most of these are now long gone, but a number of attractive amenities, such as the original roof pavilion, remain. In the basement, the laundry room, with its original gas equipment, also remains.

## *The Westmoreland*

The Westmoreland is a classic cooperative apartment house located at 2122 California Street, Northwest, in the fashionable Kalorama neighborhood, and it is another building that is featured in the *Best Addresses* book. This stately structure first opened as a premier rental building in 1906, and in 1948, after some effective preparatory work was done by its residents, the Westmoreland was converted into a cooperative. The building's residents were instrumental in taking the initiative, successfully guiding the co-op into a successful transition and sale. It has sixty apartments.

The Westmoreland, in Kalorama, was built in 1906 as an early top-tier apartment building. It became a cooperative in 1948. *Courtesy of the DC Cooperative Housing Coalition.*

At six stories tall, the Beaux-Arts building provides an impressive view of the District from its location at the crest of Kalorama Heights. The fine lobby displays an intricate mix of various marbles and retains its detailed columns. It was designed by Edgar S. Kennedy and Harry Blake and was then built by Edgar Kennedy, the developer of some of Washington's most impressive early apartment houses, including Meridian Mansions and the Kennedy-Warren. These apartment buildings that Kennedy built very often created the model and standard that was used for later luxury apartment homes in Washington, D.C.

## The 1950s and More Co-op Conversions

### *The Mendota*

Just east of Connecticut Avenue in the Kalorama Triangle neighborhood is the Mendota, one of the District's oldest luxury apartment buildings. It was constructed by builder J.L. Marshall and architect James G. Hill, the same team that built the Ontario Apartments in Lanier Heights in the following years. In 1901, at the time it was erected, the Mendota offered an upscale housing alternative to living in a row house in the District. It was the first apartment building constructed in Kalorama Triangle and sat at the corner of Twentieth Street and Kalorama Road. The Mendota was converted into a cooperative in 1952. Today, the seven-story building features forty-eight residences and offers some of the most generous floor plans found in the

The Mendota Apartment House in 1907, when the Washington Heights neighborhood was first being developed. The Mendota is well known for its fine apartments. *Courtesy of the Historical Society of Washington, D.C.*

District. The vintage brass elevator, which is still manually operated, is an interesting feature of the building. Most of the apartments have retained their various period architectural details, such as the original cornice work and well-crafted flooring. These features were very likely saved due to the building's conversion to an owner-occupied property. Preservation of such distinctive architectural details and human craftsmanship are among the added benefits of converting to a cooperative.

**James G. Hill** (1841–1913) was a noted and influential Washington, D.C. architect during the second half of the nineteenth century. Hill was born in Massachusetts and gained his architectural training with Bryant & Gilman in Boston from 1857 to 1862. After the Civil War, he went to work for the Treasury Department, which had design responsibility for the government's larger architectural projects. From 1876 to 1883, he was the supervising architect of the Department of the Treasury and oversaw projects around the country, designing or supervising the designs of a large number of courthouses, post offices and other public buildings. Many of these substantial structures were built in the weighty Romanesque Revival style and remain today as the focal points of some American cities. In Washington, D.C., he was responsible for the construction of several noted landmarks, including the Bureau of Printing and Engraving Building and the massive main building of the Government Printing Office.

After federal service, in 1884, he went into private practice and designed several graceful and solid buildings, like the Atlantic Building at 930 F Street, Northwest, and the Washington Loan and Trust Company Building, a landmarked building at the corner of Ninth and F Streets, Northwest. His experience in good, solid construction can clearly be seen in his design and supervision of the Mendota and the Ontario Apartment Houses. He was active in the national AIA until shortly before his death in 1913.

When completed, the Mendota had forty-nine apartments: twenty-three one-bedroom units, twelve two-bedroom units, seven three-

Jeannette Rankin, a resident of the Mendota, was the first female member of Congress. She is seen here in 1917. *Courtesy of the Library of Congress.*

bedroom units and seven four-bedroom units. The top floor featured a public dining room, and the ground floor contained a drugstore and a doctor's office—all are now long gone.

Prominent residents of the Mendota included its architect, James Hill, and Kalorama developer Lawrence Sands with his wife, Margaret Foyle Sands, who was one of the daughters of John Little, the "pre-subdivision" owner of the land beneath the Kalorama Triangle neighborhood. Additionally, the Mendota was home to progressive Nebraska senator George W. Norris, and to Jeannette Rankin, the first woman to serve in Congress.

## *1870 Wyoming Avenue*

A handsome and substantial structure designed by noted Washington, D.C. architect B. Stanley Simmons, 1870 Wyoming Avenue, Northwest, was built by Lester Barr, a well-respected local developer of early twentieth-century Washington. Architect Simmons (1871–1931) was a skilled designer who created more than sixty apartment houses in the city. 1870 Wyoming was completed in 1917 as a luxury rental apartment property. In 1951, it was converted from a rental to a cooperatively owned property.

The exterior of this seven-story building has a stately Beaux-Arts Classical Revival design. The twenty-eight apartments include nineteen three-bedroom units and nine two-bedroom units. There are four apartments on each floor, and two per floor have balconies. The apartments are spacious, with well-designed floor plans, and most have two bathrooms.

1870 Wyoming has been featured in several local history books and is noted for its attractive buff-brick exterior; its distinctive lobby, which features marrezzo walls (a special faux marble–type of finish); and its intricate multicolor mosaic floor. Its amenities include a roof deck with panoramic views, a front desk, bicycle storage and basement storage lockers.

Over the years, the building has been home to many government professionals and, especially, a number of military officers. For instance, marine corps general John A. Lejeune of World War I fame lived here after the war. The Marine Corps Base Camp Lejeune in North Carolina is named in his honor. Admiral John S. McCain Sr. and his family also lived here in the 1940s. He was a pioneer of aircraft carrier operations and the grandfather of the late senator John McCain.

## *The Westchester*

Another extraordinary and justly famous property is the Westchester, located at 4000 Cathedral Avenue, Northwest, not far from the National Cathedral. This attractive cluster of five buildings, with a total of 520 apartments, sits on spacious, landscaped grounds. Designed by Harvey H. Warwick Sr., it was launched as a rental property in 1931. Its principal developer was Gustave Ring of Washington, D.C., and he worked with Morris Cafritz. The Westchester became a cooperative in 1954.

The Westchester's construction began in March 1930, and the structure was designed with a plan of eight buildings laid out around an expansive quadrangle that was open to Cathedral Avenue. The financial pressures of the Great Depression permanently halted the full execution of this master plan midway through construction. Nonetheless, the five completed buildings were opened, with their apartments becoming some of the most desirable in the city. Its Tudor Revival architectural style was carefully implemented throughout the complex. There are additional touches of a Moorish feel in some of the building's exterior elements, and they are well blended together.

With its eight-building design, the Westchester was originally planned to be the largest apartment complex south of New York City. Even with its five completed buildings, the Westchester remained the largest set of luxury apartment buildings in Washington, D.C., for nearly twenty years—that is, until 1952, when the Woodner (a rental property on Sixteenth Street, Northwest, with more than 1,100 units) opened.

A dramatic presentation drawing from the architects of the Westchester that shows the planned complex. *Courtesy of the Westchester Cooperative.*

A view of the entrance to the Westchester in the mid-1950s, showing the details of the complex's notable architecture. *Courtesy of the Westchester Cooperative.*

From the Westchester's website:

> *Attractive elements of the past continue to be seen at today's Westchester. For example, there is a magnificent beech tree behind the North Main building that dates from the late 1800s, when the property was still a farm. There are Chinese screens and mirrored pillars brought in by society designer Dorothy Draper in the late 1930s and impressive Georgian gates and pillars leading into the complex, imported from an English estate that had been destroyed in World War II. Today, the Westchester's well-proportioned prewar apartments, expansive common spaces, and meticulously landscaped grounds continue to offer an excellent instance of graceful living in the nation's capital.*

As with several of the other top-level properties that were built before the Second World War, the Westchester had a public restaurant when the building opened. However, as was the case with other such properties, including co-ops, its restaurant was ultimately closed in 2016. It was the last public restaurant in Washington, D.C., to operate within a cooperative. Today, for its residents, the co-op continues to provide a fitness center, valet parking, a small grocery store, a beauty salon and a barbershop.

**Harvey H. Warwick** (1893–1972) is considered to be one of the city's most-skilled apartment building designers of his time, and he was known for his quality work and innovative designs. He planned two of the Washington, D.C. area's most significant apartment building complexes: the Westchester on Cathedral Avenue and Colonial Village in Arlington, Virginia. Harvey Warwick's apartment building designs helped influence the development of apartment building use in Washington, D.C. He was born in Kansas City, Missouri, and later worked for his uncle, an architect.

After serving in World War I, Warwick came to Washington, D.C., in 1919. Warwick's principal client from 1922 until the Great Depression collapse of the housing market was Morris Cafritz. Cafritz became one of Washington, D.C.'s most successful developers of the twentieth century. Warwick designed numerous single-family dwellings for Cafritz, successfully employing a variety of romantic and domestic styles in his plans. He also used these styles in many apartment buildings.

Warwick's finest high-rise apartment was the Westchester. In 1930, Cafritz joined in partnership with Gustave Ring to conceive the apartment complex on Cathedral Avenue, Northwest. Retaining architect Warwick, the pair intended for the Westchester to be a twenty-eight-acre project with eight connected eight-story buildings. Employing the Tudor Revival style, Warwick prepared a design that allowed every elevation to have projecting bay elements.

Working with Ring in 1935, Warwick designed Colonial Village in nearby Arlington. This pioneering garden apartment development was the first large-scale FHA apartment development in the country. The two also created Arlington Village. Overall, Warwick designed over forty apartment buildings in the Washington, D.C. area between 1922 and 1945.

Harvey Warwick also worked with builder Paul T. Stone, designing Gunston Hall Apartments in Alexandria, Virginia. At the Westchester, Warwick was a stockholder with Ring and Cafritz until they sold the complex in 1937. Additionally, he owned the noted Dunbar Hotel (now demolished) at Fifteenth and U Streets, Northwest. Harvey Warwick died in July 1972.

## *The Ontario Apartment House*

This distinctive building, which was constructed between 1903 and 1906, is well known not only for its fine Beaux-Arts architecture but also for its important role in helping create the attractive atmosphere of the Lanier Heights neighborhood. It is additionally recognized for having a long history of interesting and influential residents. The Ontario has been a co-op since 1953. Today, it continues to be a comfortable and desirable address.

The Ontario was built by Archibald M. McLachlen, a banker and real estate developer who was famously a major creator of the Lanier Heights neighborhood. For the Ontario, he envisioned something unusual: an apartment building set well back from the street, surrounded by lawns and trees and bordered by a stone wall.

The Ontario in a presentation drawing from 1906. This apartment house, when built, was out at the perimeter of the city, next to Rock Creek Park. *Courtesy of the* Washington Times, *February 18, 1906.*

For his new building, McLachlen turned to James G. Hill, who had been recently overseen the design and construction of the Mendota Apartment House. Hill designed the Ontario to be a six-story structure containing 120 apartments that now range in size from 557 to 2,195 square feet—from compact, living-room-and-bedroom homes to expansive layouts with four bedrooms, separate dining rooms and a maid's quarters. Wings project from both the front and the back of the structure. The Ontario was built in two stages and was originally intended to be named the Glenolden (on period maps, this is the name shown for the first section that was completed at the time). The building's distinctive pebble-dash stucco exterior has recently been expertly restored.

In 1983, the co-op members of the Ontario created a fascinating book, a history of their cooperative titled *The Ontario*. Along with the more mundane historical facts of the building, they covered stories of many of the residents, both early and later. The following is a brief excerpt:

> *The Ontario is a turn-of-the-century apartment house at 2853 Ontario Road, Northwest, in the Adams Morgan section of Washington, D.C. We are six stories tall, located on two acres of land and contain 120 apartments above the basement.*
>
> *At this writing, we number 147, including our manager and janitor, who live here, too. An informal survey indicates that nearly one-fourth of us are in the "senior" category (over 60 years old), about three-fourths are between twenty and sixty, and the remaining five persons are children under twelve.*

This history also reports on one of the early residents, "Mother Pickett," or Lasalle Pickett, the young wife of General Pickett from the Battle of Gettysburg. She famously lived at the Ontario from 1905 until 1929 and would, at times, hang a Confederate flag outside of her window. (It was

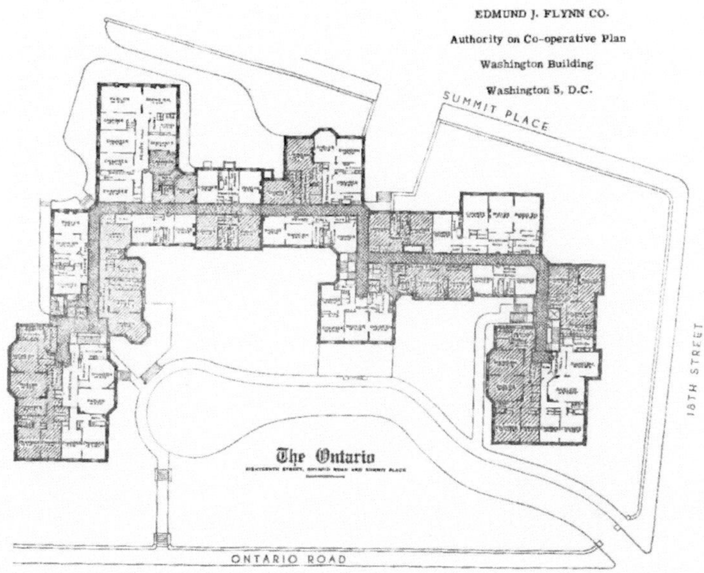


A site plan of the Ontario from the 1953 conversion that shows the layout of apartments on a typical floor. *Courtesy of the Edmund J. Flynn Company.*

A view of the original entrance of the Ontario Apartment House. The building was constructed in two stages between 1903 and 1906. *Photograph by the author.*

always taken down.) Others, like Douglas MacArthur, Nora Ephron and Carl Bernstein, were later residents. Mr. Bernstein famously stripped the interior of his large unit—every single wall—and completely changed the character of the apartment, an occasionally familiar story in many older co-op buildings. Over the years, the building has been home to many other notable residents who have worked in the fields of politics, law and government, the arts, education and medical research.

## DOWNTOWN

### *The Presidential Apartments*

The Presidential Apartments are housed in a substantial brick-and-stone structure, located in the Sixteenth Street Historic District, one of the more prominent historic districts in Washington, D.C. (There are thirty-seven such districts in the city.) Completed in 1923, this eight-story *Best Addresses* building was designed by influential D.C. architect Appleton P. Clark Jr., and it was built by Clara R. Dennis for the then-sizeable sum of $350,000. It sits at 1026 Sixteenth Street, Northwest.

One interesting note related to the construction of the Presidential is that the real estate history of Washington contains a surprising number of active women developers, architects and builders. This is a fact that is often hidden within dusty real estate documents. It is unfortunate that many of these women are not more well known and are more often noted in local histories.

Appleton P. Clark Jr. (1865–1955) designed many projects in Washington, D.C., including the Roosevelt Hotel at 2101 Sixteenth Street, Northwest, and the Riggs National Bank building on Pennsylvania Avenue near the White House. He and his firm also helped train a number of younger architects in apartment building design as the city was being developed. His influence on the look and the internal layouts of the District's early apartment houses was considerable. Clara Dennis's Presidential Apartment Building was erected by the construction firm Parsons and Hyman.

Today, the Presidential has forty-four apartments; many of the units have been upgraded, but most still retain their original character, with fine wall moldings and spacious layouts. The property is located at the corner of Sixteenth and L Streets, Northwest, just four blocks north of the White House. Several of the original residences have been combined to form larger apartments. According to the historical records of the co-op, Mrs.

The Presidential Apartments, shown here at the time of their conversion into a cooperative, in 1959. *Courtesy of the Edmund J. Flynn Company.*

Dennis named the building the Presidential because she felt that it was ideally situated to house some members of President Warren G. Harding's cabinet. At the time of the property's conversion to a cooperative, in 1959, the Edmund J. Flynn Company promoted the conversion and managed the sales of the units. After this transition, Flynn, along with his family, moved into the building and lived there for several years. (Some of this information is courtesy of the Presidential Co-op's website.)

## SOME NOTEWORTHY NEW CO-OP CONSTRUCTION WAS ALSO OCCURRING IN THE CITY

### *In Foggy Bottom*

The Foggy Bottom area became available for development in the 1950s, after the older industrial structures of the neighborhood were cleared from the land. The neighborhood, in large part, had for many years contained a number of imposing coal-gas storage tanks owned by the Washington Gas Company. The area smelled and was a loosely maintained industrial stretch. In the 1800s, its proximity to the lower end of the C&O Canal and the waterfront had made it a prime location for commercial use, but the city had matured, and this land remained, situated close to the beautiful National Mall. So, for a number of years, beginning shorty after World War II, civic efforts persisted to redevelop the area.

Following discussions in the early 1950s, a group of developers, led by George Preston Marshall (the then-owner of the Washington Redskins), purchased a large piece of the property, a tract that also included much of the land of today's Watergate Complex. The original 1954 plans for the area were impressive. It was to be named the Potomac Plaza Center, and it was set to rival some of New York City's developments in size. It was to include a luxury hotel, office buildings, a variety of housing units (including co-ops), medical buildings and public amenities. The original plan envisioned a large medical services component, but financing was an ongoing struggle. Two of the apartment buildings on the north side were designed then built, with the Edmund J. Flynn Company being brought in to market the co-op apartments as attractive upper-level homes. Because of financing issues, the full plan, of course, never materialized, but today, there are the buildings that endure, including desirable co-op homes and a number of the medical offices. The larger part of the proposed project was to have been situated south of Virginia Avenue. This land was eventually sold to the Italian developers of the Watergate.

## *Potomac Plaza Cooperative*

In 1957, after successful planning work and with sales assistance provided by the Edmund J. Flynn Company, the 274-unit Potomac Plaza Cooperative Apartments opened at 2475 Virginia Avenue, Northwest. The structure is a Mid-Century Modern apartment building located near the river in what is, at times, known as the Kennedy Center neighborhood, not far from the George Washington University campus. The building was the first to be built as a part of the ambitious plan of developer George Preston Marshall and his associates from New York. It was designed by the Washington, D.C. architectural firm of Dixon & Weppner. Frederick Wallace Dixon and Robert A. Weppner were local architects who also practiced separately in the city.

## *Potomac Plaza Terraces*

Four years after the completion of Potomac Plaza, in 1961, the nearby Potomac Plaza Terraces Apartment House was completed and opened as a cooperative. This project had initially been planned as be a co-op medical office building, but it was changed to contain apartment homes with medical suites on the first floor. Located at 730 Twenty-Fourth Street, Northwest, this ten-story, 150-unit Mid-Century Modern building has particularly attractive and functional balconies for some of its apartments. It also has a roof deck with a fine view of the Potomac River. This time, the architects came from the firm of F. Wallace Dixon and Associates, and the project was built by Magazine Brothers Construction.

Edmund J. Flynn had actively and positively promoted the sales in this project with prominent newspaper articles and advertisements. It can be reasonably noted that his work at the time laid out the facts about cooperatives in a way that created much of the good public perception of co-op ownership, which spread throughout the Washington, D.C. area. His efforts assisted in moving forward the fresh acceptance of new co-ops as being excellent homes. This likely helped advance the other co-op projects that were very shortly to occur in nearby areas. The construction of the two Potomac Plaza buildings foreshadowed the large developments that were to be built in the District in the 1960s.

# 4
# THE 1960s: COOPERATIVE LIVING CONTINUES TO EVOLVE AND THRIVE

Following the widespread economic declines that occurred in many of America's urban areas after the end of World War II, civic leaders of the 1950s engaged in much of the official—and community-level—discussion about the situation, talking and contemplating how to best plan for the future of the nation's cities. These conversations resulted in an intentional drive to revitalize some of the country's core urban areas. The ensuing efforts were oftentimes very successful, and at other times, they were done with controversy and with mixed results. The less-than-successful results included some large-scale destruction of historic areas and large-scale removal of many of the poor and racial minorities.

## SOUTHWEST

In Washington, D.C., the southwest quadrant of the city—the smallest quadrant in both population and size—was largely cleared and redeveloped in the early 1960s. The major urban development plans that were drawn up at that time fully altered the fabric of the neighborhood and were fervently debated. There were questions about what Southwest was to be, whether or not to maintain the same street configurations, possibly changing the basic principal functions of the area and changing the appearance and use of the waterfront. In the end, most of the city's comprehensive plan proceeded, which was truly large in scope and offered the District an exciting opportunity to experiment with several new and innovative architectural projects, both large and small.

During this period of development, several large residential projects were built near the Potomac River; among these were two that were planned as cooperatives and one that was later converted to cooperative ownership. The River Park Co-op was completed in 1962. Tiber Island was opened in 1965 as a rental property, and it was converted into a co-op in 1984. Harbour Square, the largest and most prominent—and the most ambitious—of all of them opened as a cooperative in 1966. Large complexes like these were able to offer a range of amenities for members, such as pools, private meeting rooms, party rooms and fitness centers.

These new projects were designed by nationally well-known Washington-area architects, including (for the three projects previously noted): Charles Goodman; Chloethiel Woodard Smith; and Keyes, Lethbridge & Condon. Their fine work contributed to the successful overall redevelopment of the area, as their attractive and convenient new complexes were desired by homeowners. They were promptly populated by an influx of residents coming to the new Southwest. In addition to these three major projects, a number of other developments were also built as condominiums, individual townhouses and rental properties.

The co-ops—Harbour Square, River Park and, later, Tiber Island—are now well-established and important residential elements in Southwest D.C.. It should be noted that, with a sensitivity toward historic preservation, several historic pieces of original housing in the area were saved and attractively incorporated into the new developments.

## Harbour Square

Today, the Harbour Square Complex continues to be the premier co-op complex in Southwest D.C., and it is among the finest in the city. Built between 1963 and 1966, it provides a good example of how Washington city planners made a deliberate attempt to attract the best architects to the city in order to show the city's residents and the world that the District was poised to move into the future. The construction of the complex—with its highly innovative design, mixed housing types and effective use of green space—was a significant step forward in the refashioning of Southwest D.C. One of the most famous early residents of Harbour Square was Vice President Hubert H. Humphrey, who moved there with his wife, Muriel, in October 1966. According to news reports, during the 1968 presidential campaign, Humphrey told his friends that, if he was elected, he and Muriel had no intention of moving out of Harbour Square to live in the White House.

From its inception, the design of Harbour Square took particular and deliberate advantage of its riverfront location, and it leveraged the advantages of this location with a subtle interplay of design elements. Its integration of historic townhouses built in the 1790s included Wheat Row as well as the Barney and Lewis Houses. This was an early effort to adaptively reuse historic buildings and make them functional components of new developments.

The Edmund J. Flynn Company worked with the real estate development firm of Shannon & Luchs (William Shannon and Frank Luchs), which did the major financing and planning of the complex. Respected builder John McShain Inc. did the construction. Architect Chloethiel Woodard Smith, along with landscape architect Daniel Urban Kiley, created the overall design of the project. Architect Smith worked with all involved on the many

A cartoon from the 1960s, with a humorous observation about co-op living, that features Harbour Square. *Courtesy of the Edmund J. Flynn Company.*

A photograph the Harbour Square presentation model with Chloethiel Woodard Smith, the architect of the complex. *Courtesy of the Library of Congress.*

details of the buildings. The Flynn Company also marketed and arranged the sales of the apartments. Together, they made Harbour Square one the city's foremost residential complexes.

Harbour Square includes a wide range of housing configurations, offering choices between 430 apartments (with 136 different floor plans of varying sizes) and 17 townhouses. Many of the townhouses and apartments have wood-burning fireplaces. Among the complex's amenities are an indoor Olympic-sized pool and gym, both overlooking the reflecting pool; a library; a car wash; an electric vehicle charging station; and a large club room with views of the Washington Channel. When completed, Harbour Square attracted a number of prominent Washingtonians. In addition to Hubert Humphrey, the complex's other famous residents included Justice Lewis Powell of the Supreme Court; Philip N. Brownstein, who was then the assistant secretary of housing and urban development; and Admiral William Radford, a former chairman of the Joint Chiefs of Staff. (Some of the material used here was adapted from Harbour Square's website.)

Harbour Square was placed in the D.C. Inventory of Historic Sites in 2013, and it is also included in the National Register of Historic Places.

**Chloethiel Woodard Smith** (1910–1992) was a renowned Modernist architect and urban planner whose work was centered in Washington, D.C. She earned her architecture degree from the University of Oregon in 1932 and later worked in a number of firms. She established her own practice in 1963. After the Second World War, she served on several civic committees that helped shape modern Washington, D.C. She was famously the architect of Harbour Square and was the sixth woman to become a fellow in the American Institute of Architects, a major honor for architects. In downtown D.C., the intersection of Connecticut Avenue and L Streets, Northwest, gained the nickname "Chloethiel's Corner" because she designed three of the four prominent office structures on the corner. Smith was called the "Leading Lady in Urban Renewal" by *Look* magazine. A famous photograph (shown here) of her examining a scale model of Harbour Square was widely circulated. Several of her projects are listed in the National Register of Historic Places.

At Harbour Square, Smith's extensive use of glass windows and balconies was widely praised. She was clearly mindful of the nearby river and its riverside. The private and public roof gardens and the upper terrace plantings help connect these high-rise apartment buildings to the earth. The Harbour Square Complex remains one of Chloethiel Woodard Smith's most important residential projects.

After Harbour Square, Smith worked on a variety of design projects, including a notable townhouse development in Reston, Virginia. Many of Washington, D.C.'s more famous architects, including Arthur Cotton Moore, worked for her firm at one time or another. By 1971, her firm had become the largest female-run architecture firm in the United States. Smith was also a member of the U.S. Commission of Fine Arts from 1967 to 1976. She died in December 1992.

For Harbour Square's development, landscape architect Daniel Urban Kiley (1912–2004) joined with architect Smith to assist her in the overall planning of the layout of the property's expansive land. His design created many fine elements, including some deliberate visual cues that draw one's eye outward and toward to the Washington Channel. One of the classic features he used was a grid of maple trees in the entrance garden. The one-acre aquatic garden and island was planted with a willow tree to provide a pleasing unity, linking the complex to the river and reflecting the sky.

## River Park Mutual Homes

Directly across the street of Harbour Square is this impressive development of glass-and-aluminum-clad homes. Located on eleven acres in Southwest's waterfront neighborhood, it consists of two conjoined high-rise buildings and several clusters of flat- and barrel-roof townhouses. River Park was built in 1962 and was designed by Charles M. Goodman. The unique exteriors of the buildings use a sizable amount of structural aluminum in a pleasing manner—not surprising, since the Reynold Metals Development Corporation was the major partner in the development and construction of the complex.

Located one block from the Waterfront Metro Station, River Park is near the Arena Stage, the Wharf and the Maine Avenue Fish Market. Notably, when it opened in 1962, it was a pioneer in residential racial integration. Welcoming integration in a new residential complex was somewhat unusual at the time; in that same year, the United States Commission on Civil Rights had issued a report that found the District's housing to be "segregated in a very real sense." (This information came from the River Park website.) This deliberate integration was a healthy aspect that occurred in many parts of the redevelopment of the Southwest neighborhood.

**Charles M. Goodman** (1906–1992) is known for his distinctive modern midcentury designs, which he created for buildings throughout the D.C. area. He deliberately avoided the Colonial Revival look that was prevalent in local residential construction in the 1960s. Goodman believed in taking a fresh look at the needs of contemporary people and their homes, and he chose to move away from designing plain historical reproductions.

Across the river, Goodman designed the original portion of National Airport and was the principle architect of the Hollin Hills neighborhood in Alexandria, Virginia. Born in New York City but raised in Chicago, Goodman attended the Illinois Institute of Technology. He moved to Washington, D.C., in 1934 to work as the designing architect of the Public Buildings Administration, and he later served as head architect at the U.S. Department of the Treasury. After World War II, he worked on homes and suburban neighborhoods, applying his modern aesthetic to thoughtful site planning. Several of his suburban developments continue to be well known today.

## TIBER ISLAND

Tiber Island Cooperative Homes was originally built in 1965 as a rental complex at Fourth and N Streets, Southwest, but it was converted into a cooperative in 1982. It is a solid and attractive part of its Southwest neighborhood. It was designed by architects Keyes, Lethbridge & Condon

Tiber Island, a modern cooperative in Southwest. *Courtesy of the DC Cooperative Housing Coalition.*

and was built in a pinwheel shape, with a large main courtyard and townhouses located in each of its quadrants. The strong, clean and modern appearance of the building's towers stands out well in the neighborhood. It consists of four nine-story towers and contains 368 apartments and 21 two- and three-story townhouses. The complex features a large central pedestrian area built over an underground garage and connecting the four towers. Its design won an American Institute of Architects Award for Multifamily Residential Design in 1966.

Tiber Island, like Harbour Square, has thoughtfully incorporated a historical structure into its design: the Thomas Law House, an early Washington landmark that was built in 1784 and is now in the National Register of Historic Places. This handsome Federalist mansion is situated in one of the southwest corners of the co-op's grounds. It was the home and social center for some of America's early leading historical figures, including Thomas Law and his wife, Eliza Parke Custis, the eldest granddaughter of Martha Washington. In March 1796, after Thomas and Eliza's marriage, the house became known as "Honeymoon House."

## Along the Potomac

### *The Watergate Complex*

The world-famous Watergate Complex is a visually prominent and culturally notable fixture in Washington, D.C. The three luxury cooperative apartment buildings, which are components of the complex, are renowned for their exceptional location and distinguished residents. Famous politicians and a number of the city's social elite, both past and present, have made the Watergate their home for decades. During various administrations, many top officials of the White House have made the Watergate their home while living in Washington. And certainly, the Watergate Complex became notoriously famous as the site of the office burglary that ultimately led to the resignation of President Richard Nixon in August 1974.

The complex is made up of six buildings in the Foggy Bottom neighborhood of the District. Sitting next to the John F. Kennedy Center for the Performing Arts and covering a total of ten acres, this group of buildings includes the three apartment houses that were designed from the start to be sold as cooperatives and were well planned as grand properties.

- Watergate East (2500 Virginia Avenue, Northwest) was completed in May 1965. As the first of the residential buildings in this exciting new complex, its 238 apartments sold briskly. (There are now 240.)

- Watergate South (700 New Hampshire Avenue, Northwest) opened in June 1968. This was the last building constructed, and it originally had 240 apartments. It now has 230; some were combined.

- Watergate West (2700 Virginia Avenue, Northwest) began construction in July 1967, and once again, the apartments sold quickly. The building was completed in August 1968. It holds 143 units.

Built between 1963 and 1971, the Watergate complex was developed by the Italian real estate firm SGI (Società Generale Immobiliare), which had purchased the land for $10 million in 1960. The chief architect of the project was the renowned Luigi Moretti. Architecturally dramatic, the unified, compelling appearance of the complex was discussed at length before it was built. Some felt that it was too flashy and that it would overshadow the nearby Kennedy Center, which was then being planned. But to most people, the six buildings of the complex turned out to be beautiful, with a distinguishing verve. The apartments are known for their fine amenities, including private rooftop terraces and fireplaces. (The old joke goes, "The Kennedy Center is the box that the Watergate came in.")

**Luigi W. Moretti** (1907–1973) was one of the more renowned Italian architects of the twentieth century. Born in Rome, he lived almost his entire life in the same apartment building. Moretti, who was regarded as a genuinely skillful and creative architect, was adept at planning and laying out larger structures. He was attuned to the use of materials and to the details of their interactions. Moretti was also well aware of structure and form, and he could be daring and dramatic while also being measured and balanced. He designed many remarkable and well-known buildings in Italy, where he was also a noted teacher and professor. The Watergate Complex is his most famous project in the United States.

His ability to craft bold modern designs that looked timeless was evident in his work at the Watergate Complex.

The construction of the Watergate was a complicated undertaking. First, there were the many zoning hurdles that had to be resolved, and since the site was near the river, it required careful engineering considerations. In addition, the many intricate curves of the structures needed precise planning. Thus, the Watergate Complex was one of the first major construction projects in the United States in which computers played a significant role in the design work. The Washington architectural firm of Fischer and Elmore worked on the overall details of planning the buildings' constructions. The general contractor for the construction of the complex was the Magazine Brothers Construction Company.

The Watergate Complex, seen in this aerial photograph from 2006. A view that is often seen by air travelers when landing at Reagan National Airport. *Image from Wikidata.*

## In Upper Northwest

### *3900 Watson Place, Northwest*

This 141-unit Mid-Century Modern property with two buildings was completed in 1960. Initially, it was opened as a luxury rental property, but it became a co-op in 1963. These two structures were designed by New York architect Harry Price, who was assisted by the local firm of Berle & Abel, and it was built on the five acres of land that lay opposite the Westchester Cooperative. That land had remained undeveloped since the 1930s. The apartments of 3900 Watson Place are notable for their large balconies that have excellent views of the city. The first-floor residents have broad patios. Today, both of these buildings continue to be quiet and desirable top-level cooperative homes.

## The Rise of Condominiums

During the early 1960s, condominiums were also introduced to the real estate market of Washington, D.C. They presented residents with another opportunity for common ownership in a multiunit building with a differently structured ownership plan. For developers, condos were often easier to set up for initial financing and marketing. Buyers were often more easily persuaded into buying apartments if they got a paper deed to their own "real estate box"—even if that box happened to be forty feet up in the air and attached to other boxes. Certainly, condominiums did not replace co-ops, nor did they add more advantages to city neighborhoods than co-ops did, but they did—and still do—provide additional home options for city residents.

5

# THE 1970s–2000s: AS COOPERATIVE LIVING MATURES, FRESH OPPORTUNITIES AND PROPERTIES DEVELOP

The city was changing. In 1973, after the discussions that took place within the previous decades, Congress finally granted the District of Columbia a proper measure of home rule, meaning the District had the right to govern itself with a fair degree of freedom. It had been ninety-nine years—almost a century—since control of the city had been taken over by Congress. In 1874, Congress had transferred operational municipal control over to a three-member commissioner type of rule. These commissioners were appointed by Congress; thus, residents had long been without democratic representation.

This welcome event of 1973 led to some operational changes in the city's government, and these changes continue to evolve today. The city's modern civic structure has allowed the city to more fully manage real estate activities, and this, of course, always affects what occurs in local urban life. In the years since home rule, the District of Columbia and its residents have weathered the financial and political challenges of the 1990s. The city has also seen a dramatic increase in population, which caused an associated need for more housing. The continuing national financial uncertainties of the past ten years have also had an effect on the city. And Washington, D.C., continues to grow.

During the mid-1970s, with a renewed national interest in urban living, Washington, D.C., experienced an influx of people who were choosing to move back into the District. The urban riots of 1968 and their damaging physical and social aftermath had caused the population to decline in many parts of the city. For the following decades, significant rethinking and continued discussion about city life at all levels focused on healing the city and determining how best to attract new residents and build needed housing.

## A Third Wave of Conversions

From the mid-1970s to the later 1980s, a number of fine rental buildings, some in neighborhoods that had experienced a rather rapid economic decline, were once again seen as attractive. Some were converted into co-ops because their residents began to see the attractiveness and convenience of home ownership in the city. In some cases, the conversions came about as the buildings were being put up for sale. A number of these conversions helped stabilize or revitalize their local neighborhoods. Several sales, such as those of Beverly Court in Adams Morgan and Madison Terrace in Brightwood, were aided in their conversions with advice and planning assistance from offices of the city's government. In a few cases, the city even provided some needed financial support.

During this time, several building owners chose to convert to co-op, and the apartment renters were often given an opportunity to help with the conversion of their building. They were given the chance to purchase their units before the rental properties they were in went up for public sale. As with the co-op creations of the 1920s, when word of a prospective co-op got around, many people took notice of the good possibilities and, especially, the special chance at home ownership. Buildings of all types, from luxury to mid-level, were converted into co-ops during this time. At least twenty-four properties were converted to cooperative ownership between 1976 and 1988. In some buildings, the work of the residents being almost "an adventure" had a beneficial effect on the enthusiastic start of these new co-ops.

Some buildings were likewise converted into condominiums during this stretch of time, but the condo conversions often involved a more minor level of participation from the existing tenants. In each case, it depended on the character of the property sale and of the willingness of the new owner to work with the existing renters.

In several cases, building owners chose to either convert or to redevelop their properties without giving the tenants any prior notice. This resulted in some situations in which the renters were summarily put out of their homes. It was a concern that led the D.C. City Council to create the "Rental Housing Conversion and Sale Act of 1980." This bill mandated that tenants in buildings going up for sale must be offered the "first opportunity" to buy the building. This act is known today as the Tenant Opportunity to Purchase Act or TOPA.

A few of the tenant-generated conversions caused discussions among co-op members about the option of limiting the resale values of the units in the new cooperative, thereby creating, basically, a limited-equity co-op. Tenants of these conversions had to consider what would be good in a social sense and then also what would be good for their own interests. They also had to look out for the long-term health of the new co-op in a practical way. In most cases, the concept of a market-rate cooperative ownership was preferred for its long-term benefits and was chosen. In any case, in a true cooperative, trying to manage the values of shares is generally not workable in any fairly applied sense when the owners are in control.

In addition to having a building owner wish to convert and sell a property, some conversions occurred simply because the tenants became unhappy with the pattern of management of their buildings, and they acted by going to the owner with a proposal.

**The Saxony** was one such case. At 1801 Clydesdale Place, Northwest, today, the Saxony is a desirable, quiet address in Adams Morgan. It was built in 1950 as a rental property and was initially developed by the Charles E. Smith Company. Designed by architect Milton Prassas, it is a good example of the International style. In 1984, the Saxony became a cooperative when its tenants joined together to gain control of the care and maintenance of their apartment homes by purchasing the building. The rules of their new co-op placed limits on rentals by specifying that, in the future, the building would be primarily owner occupied. Today, the Saxony, a solid seven-story building, has 161 apartments, ranging in size from studios to two-bedrooms. It stands on the rise of a hill in the Lanier Heights section of Adams Morgan, overlooking Rock Creek Park and the National Zoo.

The following are some representative examples of other conversions during this time period.

**The Champlain**, at 2370 Champlain Street, Northwest, is another interesting building in Adams Morgan. This smaller four-story brick structure was originally developed and built as a rental property in 1927 by G.G. Loehler, and it was designed by Claughton West, a steadily active local architect. But in 1984, in a somewhat unusual arrangement, the building's interior was gutted by a developer, and then, it was marketed as a cooperative that offered exceptional flexibility to new owners. The construction plan allowed for a prospective purchaser to select their new apartment's location and interior design within certain specific parameters. It became a thirteen-unit co-op with generously sized floor plans of two to three bedrooms each.

**The DeSoto** is one of the oldest Washington, D.C. buildings that is now a housing co-op. Located in the Logan Circle neighborhood, near downtown, it was built in 1904 by Bates Warren and was one of the earliest apartment houses that Warren developed. The five-story, thirty-one-unit structure was also one of the first large apartment houses designed by the architectural firm of Hunter & Bell. The brick-and-stone Classic Revival building stands out, situated on its corner location at 1300 Massachusetts Avenue, Northwest, near Thomas Circle. It was converted to a co-op in 1976.

The DeSoto, seen in this modern photograph, is at 1300 Massachusetts Avenue in the Logan Circle neighborhood. *Photograph courtesy of the DC Cooperative Housing Coalition.*

**2720 Wisconsin Avenue** is a midcentury-International style building located in the city's Glover Park neighborhood. This seven-story, forty-nine-unit building was built in 1941 by developer Henry Jawish and was designed by architect Joseph Abel. It was converted to member ownership in 1974. It also features a roof deck with fine views of the city.

**Beverly Court** is another building that was developed by Bates Warren, in 1915, when the Adams Morgan area was being built out. It was purchased by its tenants and became a co-op in 1979, when the property went up for sale after the death of its owner. The four-story, thirty-nine-unit structure at 1736 Columbia Road, Northwest, was designed by Hunter & Bell in a sedate Classical Revival style. The interior of the building, with its especially spacious apartments, has remained largely unaltered during its existence.

**3900 Tunlaw Road**, Northwest, is a six-story cooperative apartment house located on attractive Tunlaw Road in the Glover Park neighborhood. The building was completed in 1959 as an upper-level quality rental property, and it was converted into a co-op in 1979. The one-hundred-unit building was originally developed by Clement C. Alpert, and today, it features a number of amenities, including a roof deck and underground parking.

## 2101 Connecticut Avenue, Northwest

Situated just south of the famous Taft Bridge, this imposing and special building is on the east side of Connecticut Avenue in the Kalorama neighborhood. For the city, Connecticut Avenue, located north of Florida Avenue, is a special treasure-trove of excellent architecture—a remarkable collection of apartment buildings. And what a variety it has—beautiful, quirky, majestic and opulent. The grand structure at 2101 embodies all the best of these architectural characteristics.

This building is justly regarded as a high point of traditional upper-level living in Washington, with grand apartments in a sturdy building in Kalorama, one of the city's finest and most distinguished neighborhoods. A splendid entry lobby with front desk and concierge serves its residents. Upstairs, elegantly appointed and finely crafted apartments are some of the largest in the city, offering up to 6,400 square feet of luxury living. High ceilings, grand foyers, wide hallways, oversized windows and detailed

The exterior façade of 2101 Connecticut Avenue, Northwest, which was built in 1928. *Photograph by the author.*

The entrance to 2101, displaying some of the fanciful Gothic-style touches that embellish the building's exterior on Connecticut Avenue. *Photograph by the author.*

moldings characterize living at 2101. The property was developed by Harry M. Bralove and associates Edward C. Ernst and John McInerney. It was completed in 1928 and was opened as a rental building, catering to the top tier of society. Its design of brick and stone was done to have a modern appearance but with prominent Gothic elements. Nine stories tall, it has sixty-four apartments. It was designed by noted D.C. architect George T. Santmyers, and he was assisted by architect Joseph Abel. The building was converted into a cooperative in 1976.

Along with a front desk that is open twenty-four hours a day, residents have access to a well-appointed roof deck with panoramic views of the city. Other notable features of the building include the decorative stone lion heads on the exterior, the well-known gargoyles and guardian statues; they are all there to protect the building's roof and walls. The grand lobby includes a crystal chandelier with a sixteen-foot ceiling, marble flooring and dark wood paneling. There are three elevators, and residents can also use a large private meeting room off of the lobby (this room can also be used for private functions). There is also a fitness center and a laundry facility in the building.

During the mid-1970s, in addition to the conversions being done with older properties, there were several conversions of prominent newer structures. These included some very attractive and upscale luxury buildings, such as the Shoreham West. Typically, as with the city's older buildings, the properties were initially organized into cooperatives—often with the participation of residents—and then, their apartments were put up for sale. Usually, the building's residents, even if they were not active participants, were given the first opportunity to purchase their apartments. After that, the units were offered to outside individuals.

## Cathedral Avenue Cooperative

This handsome twelve-story mid-century building at 4101 Cathedral Avenue, Northwest, in Cathedral Heights was opened in 1963 and became a co-op in 1978. It has 145 units, including studios and one-, two- and three-bedroom apartments. The property's pool, balconies and ribbon windows make for light-filled rooms, and these are among its nicer features. The rear of the property abuts Glover Archbold Park, where it drops down a hillside that enabled the construction of additional floors facing the park. The development of the property and its later conversion were carried out by Stuart Bernstein and John Mason. The noted Washington architectural firm of Corning, Elmore and Fischer designed the structure.

## SHOREHAM WEST

The Shoreham West Cooperative is a truly extraordinary building, a beautiful residential structure with elegant apartments. It was planned in 1963 by developer Harry Bralove, who had also built the adjacent and grand Shoreham Hotel in 1930. The Shoreham West is located at 2700 Calvert Street, Northwest, in the Massachusetts Avenue Heights neighborhood and is a solid eight-story, sixty-unit building. It was designed by the prominent New York firm of Emery Roth & Sons, along with local D.C. architect Vlastimil Koubek as an associate. The building demonstrates just how good mid-century architecture could be when done with care. At the time that it opened in 1965, developer Harry Bralove and his wife, Alice, chose to make the Shoreham West their home. In 1974, Bralove, while working with building residents, decided to convert the property into

The Shoreham West Cooperative is an elegant building that overlooks Rock Creek Park. *Photograph courtesy of the DC Cooperative Housing Coalition.*

a cooperative. For some time, Alice Bralove has held forth as the doyenne of the co-op.

The Shoreham West is among Washington's finest addresses, with splendid apartments that have generously proportioned rooms. It contains a range of floor plans, from one bedroom to a very spacious four bedrooms. The building's lobby is a graciously attractive element, and it was crafted with personal attention to detail by the Braloves. The co-op is, of course, included in James Goode's *Best Addresses*.

Harry Bralove was an exceptional developer of special buildings. His good ability, his wit and understanding of how luxury homes should be built all helped him stand out. The three names 2101 Connecticut, the Broadmoor and the Shoreham West prove this point.

## Van Ness North Cooperative

Located at 3001 Veazey Terrace in the Forest Hills neighborhood of Northwest D.C., this 461-unit property was built in 1967 as a rental building, and it was converted into a co-op in 1979. It is one of three apartment buildings and a commercial building that comprise the Van Ness Centre complex, which was built on an eighteen-acre parcel of land. Van Ness North became a cooperative apartment building that originally consisted of 466 units; a few of the units have since been combined. It is sixteen stories tall and was built into the side of a hill, allowing for variety in the landscaping. The building was designed by the architectural firm of Abel and Weinstein and consists of efficiencies and one-, two- and three-bedroom units, many of which have balconies or terraces. There are three levels of underground parking, providing space for approximately five hundred cars.

The complex was built in the modern International style by developer Robert I. Silverman. This is a building style that was famously championed by architect Joseph Abel. Constructed between 1964 and 1970, the entire complex was created at a cost of $50 million. (Some of this material was adapted from the Van Ness North Cooperative's website.)

THE CO-OPS THAT FOLLOW are further examples of conversions at this time.

**The Arundel Cooperative** is a sturdy brick Classical Revival building at 516 A Street, Northeast, on Capitol Hill that was built in 1916 by developer Thomas W. Smith, who was also recorded as the building's architect. The three-story building has twenty apartments and was converted into a co-op in 1980.

**Copley Plaza Cooperative**, located at 1514 Seventeenth Street, Northwest, in East Dupont Circle is an attractive six-story brick building that was constructed in 1917 by Harry Wardman and was designed by architect Albert M. Schneider in the sedate and attractive Georgian English style. It was opened as a rental property but was converted to co-op in 1981, when the residents came together to purchase the building after it went up for sale. The building contains 109 apartments.

**1869 Mintwood Place, Northwest,** is a quiet, attractive fourteen-unit building in Adams Morgan. This co-op was built in 1917 by Berkeley L. Simmons and was designed by local architect Merrill Vaughn. Vaughn designed many smaller apartment houses throughout the mid-city areas of the District. The building is a brick Classical Revival structure with a bit of an Edwardian English appearance. It was converted into a cooperative in 1981.

**Madison Terrace**, at 1365 Kennedy Street, Northwest, in the Brightwood neighborhood, is a six-story, forty-four-unit brick building that was built in 1936 in the mid-century Stripped Classical style. It was designed by architect Harvey P. Baxter. Later, in 1983, the residents came together to buy their building when it went onto the market, and they created the cooperative. Since then, the co-op has been home to a healthy mix of single individuals, couples and families—a diverse group from all backgrounds and income levels.

**1832 Biltmore Street, Northwest**, is an Adams Morgan co-op with intricate Beaux-Arts details that was designed by architect Nicholas R. Grimm and built by Harry Wardman in 1907. This five-story building of twenty-five units was converted into a co-op in 1984. It has a pleasing Old-World charm and a private garden.

**3025 Ontario Road, Northwest**, is a five-story yellow-brick structure that was built in the International style. It was completed in 1949 and contains forty-five apartments. It was designed by architect Leon Brown for Meyer Seigel, and it was meant to be a modern stylish building with iconic corner windows. It sits in the Lanier Heights neighborhood, near Rock Creek Park, and it was converted into a co-op in 1986.

**1820 Clydesdale Cooperative**, located in Lanier Heights on Clydesdale Place, is an attractive Beaux-Arts building that was developed by Charles D. Sager and designed by architect George T. Santmyers. The four-story building was completed in 1927 and was converted into a co-op in 1987. It has fifty-eight apartments and is not far from the National Zoo.

**711–721 Hamlin Street Cooperative**, located in Northeast D.C., had a somewhat unusual conversion, since the co-op consists of several distinct two-story buildings. These solid brick row houses near Catholic University were built in 1937 by Dallas Grady and were designed by George T. Santmyers. This group of buildings contains nineteen apartments. It became a cooperative in 1987.

**The Haddington** is an attractive building situated at 1840 Biltmore Street, Northwest, in the Kalorama Triangle neighborhood. It is a good example of the fine architecture that was commissioned in the early 1900s. Built in 1915 by developer Berkeley L. Simmons, it has sixteen apartments and became a co-op in 1987. It was designed by George N. Ray, a local architect who created a number of extraordinary homes in the Kalorama Circle area.

Overall, this period of renewed activity in the city, starting just after 1975 with people moving back into older neighborhoods, was certainly a positive time. These new cooperatives allowed many D.C. residents to purchase a home in the city and lay down roots (and this allowed them to become aware and involved Washingtonians). This interest in the city continues today, and the city continues to grow. It is logical to believe that some of this good civic appreciation of Washington, D.C., and the growth in its population was likely due in part to the existing, desirable cooperatives and to the growing numbers of co-op conversions.

In addition, during this time, there were several new projects being developed in the city that were planned and built as co-ops. One such building was the Westhaven at Twenty-Third and M Streets, Northwest, in the West

End neighborhood. Completed in 1981, it has forty-four co-op units—both one- and two-bedroom units—and it was designed in a modern style, using brick and concrete. With a first floor of commercial businesses, including the West End, a local movie theater, it is a good and valued component of its neighborhood.

## CO-OP PROJECTS IN THE YEARS AFTER 2000

In the opening years of the twenty-first century, there were just a couple of new co-op developments in the city. These low numbers were likely due to the fact that creating a condominium building often appeared to be an easier task for developers. For example, while marketing a condo project, a developer may be able to maintain more control over the building's common areas. But co-ops are definitely still a workable option.

**Capitol Hill Tower Cooperative** is the newest building to be planned and constructed as a co-op. Sitting south of the U.S. Capitol, it was completed and opened in 2006. Located at 1000 New Jersey Avenue, Southeast, near the southeast riverfront and the Nationals Baseball Stadium, this is an attractive, modern 344-unit structure that also has a separate retail commercial section on the street-level ground floor.

## A RECENT CONVERSION

### *The Chastleton*

At 1701 Sixteenth Street, Northwest, this impressive, historic white Gothic Revival structure was first completed in 1920, but it was then promptly doubled in size to a total of 310 units. For years, it was a fashionable city address, containing efficiencies and one- and two-bedroom apartments. The eight-story building was developed by the S.W. Strauss Company and was built by the Wire-Granit Construction Company. It was designed by architect Philip M. Julien. Situated on an acre of land at Sixteenth and R Streets, Northwest, it has had a variety of owners over the years.

In 1926, Harry Wardman purchased the property and converted one-quarter of the building's units into hotel rooms. They all eventually returned

At 1701 Sixteenth Street in Northwest, near Dupont Circle, the Chastleton stands out. *Photograph courtesy of the DC Cooperative Housing Coalition.*

to being rental apartments. For many years, especially through the Great Depression, some members of Congress had their city homes there. Much later, in 1984, after falling on hard times, the complex closed. But then, following two years of rehab work with city assistance, it reopened as a rental building, with a portion of its apartments being set aside for low-income tenants. In 2007, the building was again renovated and was converted into a market-rate cooperative. Today, it is a prominent element of the DuPont East neighborhood and offers its members amenities such as a roof deck and a ballroom.

# 6

# COOPERATIVE HOUSING ASSOCIATIONS AND THEIR ACTIVITIES

From the very beginning of the creation of modern cooperatives in Washington, there have been individuals and associations interested in sharing ideas and experiences about their city homes. In the 1920s, the Flynn Company became a central source for information and at times published brochures and articles about co-ops. Also, early on, the Warren Brothers, the noted co-op builders, created a newsletter titled the *Latch Key*, which circulated among their developments. Then too, over the years, individual co-op buildings, and larger complexes, have often worked together to help each other, with constructive advice and shared recommended operating practices.

## THE DC COOPERATIVE HOUSING COALITION

Today, the DC Cooperative Housing Coalition is the only organization exclusively devoted to advancing and promoting the interests of the owners of more than 150 cooperatives, comprising approximately 15,000 co-op units in the District of Columbia.

Since its founding in 1984, the coalition has existed for the dual purpose of advancing the common interests of the District's market-rate housing co-op associations and promoting them as a desirable form of home ownership. The coalition is an advocacy organization that articulates the interests of its member cooperatives before Washington, D.C.'s government officials and regulatory agencies. It is a service organization that provides information and education to its members. These services include a website, a periodic newsletter and timely seminars on topics of use to co-ops.

# A HISTORY

## *The Earlier Association*

The DC Cooperative Housing Coalition has its origins in an earlier group. A small group of co-op owners, representing twelve cooperatives, met on October 27, 1976, at the Ontario Cooperative, to establish the Cooperative Housing Association (CHA). In an article that appeared in the November 13, 1976 edition of the *Washington Post*, the association's newly elected president, David Hunter, explained, "Apartment cooperatives face certain legal and financial problems not shared by condominiums or single-family housing." A similar article appeared in the *Uptown Citizen*.

The twelve cooperatives represented, each located in the Adams Morgan and Dupont Circle North neighborhoods, were 1661 Crescent Place, 1623 Lanier Place, 1832 Biltmore Street, 1870 Wyoming Avenue, 2707 Adams Mill Road, the Lambert (1791 Lanier Place), the Lehigh (2605 Adams Mill Road), the Netherlands (1852 Columbia Road), the Northumberland (2039 New Hampshire Avenue), the Ontario (2853 Ontario Road), Rutland Court (1725 Seventeenth Street) and the Stafford (1789 Lanier Place). As of January 1977, four additional cooperatives from the same Northwest neighborhoods joined the association: 2101 Connecticut Avenue, the Altamont (1901 Wyoming Avenue), the Mendota (2220 Twentieth Street) and Cavanaugh Court (1526 Seventeenth Street).

Comparing notes, representatives from these cooperatives concluded that they shared similar issues, which, if they worked collectively, might be solved. The association's existence coincided with the city obtaining home rule in 1974, which meant District residents were empowered to represent their own interests. With the city council now responsible for local legislation, coupled with the introduction of condominiums only ten years earlier, co-ops needed to ensure that their specific interests were considered and protected.

Among the association's goals was securing institutional financing for individuals interested in purchasing cooperative units (similar to loans available in New York City under special legislation). At that time, neither banks nor savings and loan associations (S&Ls) could make mortgage loans for individual cooperative units. Specifically, federally chartered banks and S&Ls were prohibited from making loans or mortgages for individual co-op units because the individual units are not considered real estate (all Washington, D.C. S&Ls were federally chartered). To address the issue, the association worked with the Metropolitan Savings and Loan League, a trade association of twenty-two savings and loan institutions in the D.C. metropolitan area, including fifteen in the District of Columbia, and city councilmember David Clarke (D-Ward 1), who represented the Adams Morgan area.

The largest achievement of the association was the passage of the "District of Columbia Cooperative Housing Association Proportionate Voting Act of 1984" by the city council. That act allowed housing cooperatives to have proportional voting and to follow their bylaws and the laws of their organizing jurisdiction in matters of internal governing procedures.

The association continued to work on cooperative-related matters, such as real estate tax assessments and requirements for some co-ops to register as foreign corporations when doing business in D.C. However, by 1982, the association no longer held regular meetings because of waning interest. It was agreed that the organizational structure would be maintained and that meetings would be called when there were important issues of general interest to consider.

## *A New Association Arises: The Housing Coalition*

By 1984, several cooperatives recognized that in order to mobilize when an urgent matter needed to be addressed, a more formal and permanent organization was needed. Efforts to mobilize took a significant amount of time in a period that was limited to landline phones and postal mail. In that year, the DC Cooperative Housing Coalition was established. C. William "Bill" Tayler, the coalition's first legal counsel and a partner in the firm of Sachs, Greenebaum and Tayler, was instrumental in establishing the coalition. Tayler, a co-op owner himself, represented several newer and larger cooperatives that wished to establish an organization based on the association's principles. Then, as now, the coalition advanced the common interests of cooperative associations and promoted cooperative housing as a desirable form of home ownership. It served as both an advocacy organization that articulated the interests of members before government officials and regulatory agencies and as a service organization that provided information and education to its members.

Today, membership is open to all market-rate housing cooperatives in Washington, D.C., regardless of size. A volunteer board of directors, elected by member co-ops, governs the coalition. At least five seats on the board must be filled by representatives of cooperatives with fifty or fewer units. The coalition's activities are primarily funded through annual dues. The coalition was incorporated on May 24, 1993, as the DC/CHC Inc., an IRS section 501(c)(6) nonprofit organization in the District of Columbia. (Note: Because the coalition was not itself a cooperative, it could not use the word "cooperative" in its name and had to use the acronym in order to incorporate.) The primary reason for incorporating was to demonstrate to the city council that the coalition was a serious and permanent organization. Among its stated purposes in its articles of incorporation was that it would promote the concept of cooperative housing as a desirable and beneficial form of homeownership and that it would be a single force to protect the common interests of cooperative housing associations in the District of Columbia through education, research and lobbying.

The coalition's most important accomplishment occurred only a few years after it was formed. The passage of the Cooperative Housing Procedure Act of 1988 (D.C. Law 7-205) provided a uniform procedure and an equitable formula to assess real property owned by cooperatives, something the CHA had started working on twelve years earlier. Until that time, the District did not have a prescribed method to estimate a cooperative building's fair market value. Consequently, assessments were often arbitrary and unpredictable. Unfortunately, in 2010, the coalition was unable to prevent the city from requiring all co-op unit sales to be recorded and a transfer tax applied; this was an ongoing battle that the earlier association had struggled with since 1976.

The coalition successfully opposed a move by the District to annually charge each cooperative association three dollars per unit to fund a new government agency to oversee cooperatives and condominiums. The coalition also testified before the city council in support of a recycling tax credit in lieu of the city collecting recyclables, and it successfully opposed a 50 percent reduction in the trash collection tax credit, which co-ops and condominiums receive in lieu of the city collecting their trash.

At the heart of many of these efforts was the defense of cooperatives before the city council to maintain parity between cooperative homeowners and single-family homeowners, rather than treat co-ops as rental or commercial complexes. Although the coalition could not dissuade the city from using sales data to implement a new sales transfer tax in 2010, it has, over the years, succeeded in defending the valuation and assessment method prescribed by the 1988 Procedures Act that it had worked so hard to put in place.

One of the most important benefits coalition members receive is timely information. The coalition has conducted seminars and issued newsletters covering topics as diverse as elevators, rentals, taxes and oil and gas bulk purchasing agreements, among others, thus enabling members to receive information that allows them to anticipate and address changes that affect their operations.

The coalition has cohosted mayoral candidate forums and recognized council members who work on behalf of the interests of housing cooperatives. It has promoted public awareness and interest in co-op ownership by sponsoring events. It has worked with the Smithsonian Associates in conducting day-long tours of several D.C. housing cooperatives, first in 1995 to mark the seventy-fifth anniversary of the first housing co-op in the District and again in 2004. However, the planned 2020 tour to celebrate the one-hundredth anniversary had to be canceled due to the COVID-19 pandemic. In addition to supporting this book, the coalition commissioned a professionally developed fifteen-minute video (available on YouTube) documenting the one-hundred-year history of housing co-ops in D.C., *THE GOOD LIFE: 100 Years of Housing Cooperatives in Washington, D.C., 1920–2020.* The Coalition thanks the sponsors who have generously supported its activities for the centennial.

## NATIONAL COOPERATIVE BANK (NCB)

In 1978, a new banking corporation entered the world of real estate and of housing cooperatives when the National Cooperative Bank (NCB) was created. Congressionally chartered as a cooperative bank by the National Consumer Cooperative Bank Act of 1978, NCB became an active and beneficial part of the real estate world, both locally and nationally. It continues to offer banking products and services to cooperatives, their members and social organizations throughout the country.

The bank was created to address the financial needs of an underserved market. It serves as an advocate for America's cooperatives and their members, and it places particular emphasis on meeting the needs of communities that are economically challenged. To that end, NCB has also focused on community revitalization projects. The use of the cooperative model in developing a variety of businesses can certainly be healthy for communities. Modern healthcare and other social activities can be helped through ideas of co-op planning.

For more than forty years, NCB has worked with housing cooperatives, condominiums and homeowner associations, offering a range of banking services. In Washington, D.C., the bank is a well-regarded institution, and it is known for its progressive advocacy of beneficial housing policies in our society. Nationally, it continues with its promotion of good housing for people in all levels of society.

# 7
# 2020

For the last one hundred years, cooperatives have had a positive effect on Washington, D.C.'s domestic life and have had a steady appeal to many of the city's residents. The term *cooperative* is definitely an old and useful one, and it is seen in many areas of our society. Co-ops of all sorts are important parts of our world. Very broadly, the word *co-op* has grown to encompass a wide range of well-intentioned and beneficially constructive enterprises. It is very American. Today, there are an estimated twenty-nine thousand cooperatives of all types operating in every segment of the American economy.

Now, as the twenty-first century progresses, housing co-ops are solidly in place throughout our country, in cities all across the nation, with the larger numbers still concentrated in the three historically "co-op" cities: New York, Washington, D.C., and Chicago. New York alone holds about 30 percent of all the United States' housing cooperatives. *What will come in the next one hundred years?*

Of course, no one knows for sure, but a number of the civic leaders and co-op developers who worked in this field in the past one hundred years were thinking ahead and offered ideas and projects for our society. In 1957, in an interview with the *Washington Post*, Edmund J. Flynn outlined some of his ideas for "self-sufficient, moderately priced cooperative communities" with expansive grounds and amenities, and co-op stores for the residents. Others have continued to propose similar concepts. These are ideas that hold up, and they might be considered again in the future, especially as environmental concerns become increasingly important.

A building's character is initially set by the developer and the architect, the people who create the physical structure and design the home's collection of features. Construction workers and finishers then carry out the plans and add the details. But it is the building's residents, both the prominent and the not-so-prominent, who have the big, final effects on the overall character that is created in and around the property.

## The Residents of Washington's Co-ops

Because of its premier position as the nation's capital, Washington, D.C., exists and operates as a vital major city, one that is home to many notable and prominent people. A number of the city's co-ops are justly proud of the variety of their past and present more notable members. Today, co-ops all over the city have residents who are now keeping the city—and the country—functioning.

With District residents in general, one of the recent notable events within the city's many co-ops and in the city itself has been the return of families with children back into the urban areas, with some families moving into co-ops. Additionally, "empty-nesters" and retirees are moving back to the city to enjoy its many restaurants, museums, parks, bike paths and mass transit systems. Washington, D.C., is among the nation's large cities that have usefully high "walkability" scores. In the city itself, some longtime residents who have been single-home owners are now choosing to move into co-ops and stay in the District.

## The Cooperative World Today

In our present-day culture, so much is in flux. The issue of housing for today's citizens—in all levels of society—is vitally important. It is worthwhile to keep in mind that the housing cooperative model is a well-proven, time-tested and sensibly conceived method of providing desirable and environmentally smart homes. With an eye toward future planning, our city and our nation might do well to consider how co-ops can usefully fit into plans for new housing.

The co-ops of Washington, D.C., continue to thrive, and the future looks good for them. An interesting point that is being seen by co-ops all over the city is that young people and young families have chosen to move into the city and its cooperatives. Bringing active, educated and happy families to a community is always good for a city. It is important to note, too, that multiunit buildings are, in general, much more efficient than spread-out single-family properties. This is a crucial consideration as we sensibly plan out a national energy policy for the future. Additionally, co-ops often inspire member involvement in their local communities, and co-op members often try to look out for what is best for the city.

For housing in our dynamic world, our city could decide that it would be smart to create some new cooperatives with real and regular equity ownership that would be beneficial to co-op members. This would be an effective method of allowing younger and newer citizens to become vested homeowners. It could possibly be done with the city assisting some private developers in areas of the city where development would be beneficial.

Presently, in the city, there are a number of limited-equity co-ops, and some are contending with management issues, and keeping their residents engaged in operations. Perhaps a new civic umbrella organization, basic, without other motives, could be set up by the city to help them. Some of these limited-equity co-ops have, in fact, been moving toward financially stronger operating configurations, and several are allowing their co-op members to partake in the actual equity value of the co-op properties. One such example is the Parkchester, a garden apartment development in Anacostia, Southeast, with 128 units, which has recently chosen to remove its controlled-equity policies and is now moving to publicly sell its apartment-shares.

The real-world history that has been collected by cooperatives is important and can be useful. In fact, a number of condominiums have recently been taking a look at how co-ops are generally run, with the idea of adopting what has effectively worked. They are inspecting the rules and procedures that most co-ops use to manage their buildings as smoothly as possible, so that they might be able to better deal with their own chronic problems. Thus, some condos have employed a number of these operating procedures after noting that they make good sense.

# 8
# SOME FACTS ABOUT A COOPERATIVE'S OPERATION

## LIVING IN THE MODERN WORLD

### *What Are the Details of a Co-op? And How Does It Differ from a Condo?*

To review: A housing cooperative is a form of ownership in which a person purchases shares of stock or some other form of membership in a corporation that was specifically formed for the purpose of providing its members with a place to live. Here are some more facts.

*In what ways is this different from a condominium?* One basic difference is that, while the ownership of a condominium unit constitutes direct ownership of real property, ownership in a cooperative constitutes a share ownership in a corporation. It is the corporation that has the ownership—fee simple title—of the entire property, the real estate, buildings and land. The ownership interest of the members in their residence is an ownership of personal property. The specific method of this ownership can vary from co-op to co-op. Some co-ops issue shares of stock and a proprietary lease; others do not issue stock but, instead, offer some form of ownership contract. In either case, the purchaser becomes a member of the cooperative and, as such, gains exclusive occupancy rights to a specific building unit as well as the use and enjoyment of the cooperative's common elements.

Condominium ownership, in contrast, combines real property ownership—fee simple—of the individual condo unit with an interest as "tenants in common" in all of the common areas and facilities of the association. This common area ownership is shared equally among association members.

Another major difference between co-ops and condos is in how real estate taxes are assessed and paid. For co-ops, taxes are assessed on the entire cooperative as a whole, not on individual units. The tax is paid by the corporation, but the proportionate share for each unit is passed on to the individual unit owner as part of the monthly fee. For condos, the local government assesses and bills each unit individually, and unit owners pay the assessed tax directly to the government.

In practice, the newer condominium legal concept came into general use in the early 1960s in neighborhoods throughout the Washington, D.C. area—as well as in other regions—as American cities were being rebuilt and expanded. It seems that some developers of new buildings and new projects often decided that it was easier to market and sell discrete pieces of real estate, boxes in the air, rather than more fully consider the overall end result and how their projects might exist in the future.

Although these two forms of home ownership are outwardly similar, in practice, they differ in some respects. The operational organization of many co-ops has, over the years, evolved to effectively and fairly deal with life in a multiunit building. Many condos are fully successful, but frequently, this success is due to the extraordinary effort given by some good and persistent individuals. The co-op arrangement offers a structure that will usually more easily permit a building to thrive. Some owners like the laissez-faire practices that many condos have, but this method of operation can, at times, lead to situations like unexpected special assessments. The basic concept of a co-op puts the long-term health of the association front and center so that there is an organization in place that can wisely consider the overall shared best interests of the group. Thus, operational issues, such as allowing unit rentals, can be better decided on and managed.

Regarding the physical upkeep of the property and the management of reserve funds, the co-op model can make it simpler to promote the good decisions needed to keep the property properly functioning and maintained. It may also allow the group to more easily discuss the various ideas that usually arise concerning building use. At times, nonresident owners may not have the same financial concerns as homeowner residents. Dealing with an absentee owner, in either a co-op or a condo, can often be complicated.

# THE ELEMENTS OF A TYPICAL CO-OP'S OPERATION

As with any democratic group, the co-op association's members work together and delegate operating authority. Thus, the cooperative's board of directors is charged with directing the regular operations and business affairs of the co-op. For instance, the board adopts an annual budget to meet the estimated expenses for the coming year, including the co-op's real estate taxes. The board also has the authority to establish, amend and enforce the cooperative's house rules that, together with the bylaws and the proprietary lease or other ownership documents, govern a members' use and occupancy of the property.

Although some cooperatives may be entirely self-managed, many, if not most, contract with a property management firm or have an in-house professional manager to handle such matters as the maintenance and repair of the common property, the hiring and supervision of staff, the collection of monthly assessments or other fees due to the co-op, the payment of bills and bookkeeping. As with all multiunit buildings, effective supervision is a

The Netherlands Cooperative has a side yard garden spot. *Photograph by the author.*

key aspect of proper co-op operation. Correctly dealing with problems and people is vital and sometimes difficult.

In addition to participating in annual and special meetings, electing fellow members to the board of directors and serving on the board (if elected), members of the co-op can participate in the operation of the co-op in other ways. There are various committees and special projects to work on, and there are all types of related activities that might be initiated; for example, a grounds committee may have members interested in gardening. Most co-ops typically have a person or two, familiar people, who are always ready to plan a party or special event.

## EXPENSES: FEES AND ASSESSMENTS

Monthly assessment fees for each cooperative unit are calculated to cover that unit's proportionate share of the cooperative's expenses as based on the number of shares of stock or the percentage of ownership that is otherwise connected to that unit. These shares or percentages are set at the time the cooperative is established and remain fixed. Included in the monthly fees are the regular costs for operating and maintaining the cooperative: management company fees, employee wages and benefits, the cooperative association's insurance, underlying mortgage (if any), shared master-meter utilities and common area utilities, contributions to reserves, real estate taxes and other regular expenses.

Establishing co-op fiscal reserves is an important task, as is properly maintaining the reserves. As with any home, reasonably anticipating and then being able to pay for needed maintenance is vital. And at other times, a co-op may decide to undertake a building improvement and will then budget for that cost. Most co-ops plan an annual budget that includes all expected expenses for the year. But occasionally—just as they occur in condominiums—additional special (sometimes sudden) assessments may be required to meet an expense that cannot be met through the regular monthly assessments or by drawing from reserve funds. Whether such special assessments are needed or used varies among cooperatives.

In comparing fees with other cooperatives, it should be noted that there are always variations in the kinds of services (desk staff, on-site management or maintenance staff) and facilities (gyms, pools, laundry rooms and such) that are provided. There are also differences in what utilities might be master metered and included in the monthly assessment and in what utilities and services might be chosen and paid for by individual apartments. Each co-op is unique, but one of the benefits of the friendly interchange of ideas is the sharing of experiences and learning what works best.

# 9

# BEFORE OUR MODERN WORLD: A LOOK AT THE EARLIER GROWTH OF THE COOPERATIVE HOUSING CONCEPT

The following is an examination of the early history of the idea of housing cooperatives.

## Earliest Times

Along with the examples of ancient castles, where the structures were often shared by extended families, we also have a variety of recorded instances from all over the world of friends and associates joining together to "share the roof" of a building. These were frequently crafted with one apartment per floor and were legally accepted by the "city officials" in various locales; they were practical and sensible. In ancient Rome, the *Digest of Justinian* described cases of separate and legal home ownerships within a larger structure but with the shared possession of a common roof. This shared proprietorship, then as now, was almost automatically important because it created a healthy vested self-interest among all the individuals involved. That is, it established a direct concern to have the property correctly built and then properly maintained.

Throughout mankind's later history, almost whenever and wherever people chose to congregate and create a town or community, individuals have regularly continued to pool their resources and pragmatically build shared homes. So, as the more technically constructed and complex cities emerged, the wisdom and usefulness of this practice of sharing became more evident.

# In the Nineteenth Century

Historically, the more modern co-op models, ones that we are commonly familiar with today, arose in Europe during the nineteenth century. In large part, we draw many of our common understandings of cooperatives from the projects and plans that were developed in England and mainland Europe during those years. With a reasonable historic perspective, we can also perceive the way in which co-ops were typically viewed and wanted back then. The famous English worker co-ops of the mid-1800s had several origins, from the self-motivated, progressively inspired projects of self-interested groups, to the cases of enlightened owners planning some decent worker housing.

These worker developments were often broad-ranging concepts in which housing was definitely an important element, but such arrangements may have also typically included additional aspects, such as financial and general provisioning. These are usually cited as the foundations of our present-day cooperatives. Less often noted, but still occurring at that time, were the instances in which wealthy individuals and families chose to join together, making plans to combine their resources and more effectively deploy their assets in order to create enjoyable homes with housing cooperatives.

Robert Owen (1771–1858) is considered by many to be one of the originators of the modern cooperative movement. He was a Welshman who made his fortune in the cotton trade, and he famously believed in the idea of putting his workers in a good environment with access to education for themselves and their children and decent housing. Owen successfully put his forward-thinking concepts into effect at the cotton mills of New Lanark, Scotland, which he (and other investors) acquired in 1799. It was there, in the early 1800s, that many of the first modern cooperative innovations were set up: stores, education, villages and housing.

Certainly, too, there is the famous Rochdale Society of Equitable Pioneers, which was founded in 1844 as an early member cooperative; its influence deserves to be noted. Although other cooperatives had preceded it, the Rochdale Cooperative became the prototype for a number of societies in Great Britain. Its members thoughtfully discussed their ideals and their plans. The Rochdale Pioneers are most well known for formulating the Rochdale Principles, a set of objectives for cooperation, principles which have provided the operating foundations that are now used by many co-ops and communes around the world. Today, the updated principles include:

- Voluntary and open membership.
- A democratic control.
- Member economic participation.
- Education and information.
- A concern for community.

Into the latter half of the 1800s, co-ops of all manner arose in England. In 1863, the North of England Cooperative Society was created, comprising about three hundred various types of co-ops, including homes. In 1895, the International Cooperative Alliance was established, and today, it is thriving globally as a widely recognized organization in the worldwide cooperative movement. Additionally, toward the end of that century, housing co-ops in most other European countries were being developed, especially in France and Finland. Some of these co-ops served as general models for the legal and financial arrangements of the new cooperatives that were soon to be created in America.

In examining Germany in the mid- to late nineteenth century as a representative example of activity in other nations, some of the housing cooperatives that were initially established there were no doubt influenced by British endeavors. An early homeownership-based housing cooperative was founded in 1862 in Hamburg. Later, Germany's adoption of its new Co-operative Act in 1889 (which helped define legal issues and liabilities) led to a further expansion of co-op housing development.

Much later, after World War II, the acceptance and use of housing cooperatives with positive approval greatly expanded throughout Europe, especially during the progressive times of the 1960s and 1970s. Today, co-ops there remain popular, particularly within northern European nations, and they are rightly seen as environmentally sound methods of urban living. Throughout the present-day world, cooperatives in all varieties, including housing, are increasingly seen to be practical and beneficial creations.

## Looking at the United States

In the latter half of the 1800s, within a fair number of America's cities, an assortment of specifically created single-purpose housing cooperatives were organized and built. These were done for a variety of reasons, usually well-considered and sensible ones. Some were built by unions for their member workers. This housing concept of union-provided homes was continued into the twentieth century, especially in the New York City area, where a number of large complexes were designed and built by prominent unions. Today, these sturdy cooperatives are carrying on, offering good homes for union members and other citizens of their city. In 1927, the Amalgamated Clothing Workers of America constructed its first cooperative in the Bronx. And in the late 1960s, the same union built Co-op City, one of the largest U.S. cooperatives, and it was also located in the Bronx. Today, Co-op City is home to more than fifteen thousand residents.

Historically, some religious groups and other societies have also, on occasion, developed housing cooperatives to provide homes for their members or to provide some general community assistance. In addition, a variety of co-ops were envisioned and built by particular cultural and ethnic groups, usually as distinct, specially conceived constructions. One notable example of this was the housing cooperative developed by Finnish artisans in 1918; they created the Finnish Home Building Association in Brooklyn, New York.

Meanwhile, among the upper levels of society in New York City, just after the turn of the twentieth century, the luxury housing market was growing for the very wealthy people who worked in the financial district. To meet that interest in the luxury housing market, a small number of experienced real estate planners developed and built several elaborate housing cooperatives between 1910 and 1920. These were especially created as large and well-crafted homes in shared buildings, and they were sold to interested and affluent individuals. Most of these have continued on as co-ops to the present day, and they stand as distinctive and historic works of urban art and as comfortable homes for their co-op members. Among them is the Dakota, which was built in 1882; it is located in the Central Park West neighborhood and has been home to such luminaries as John Lennon, Leonard Bernstein, Judy Garland, Gilda Radner and Rudolf Nureyev—to name just a few.

On another track, in late nineteenth-century America, many community-improvement concepts were being put forth progressively, with the "co-op" designation and home building being one of them. In a number of towns, savings and loan associations arose, and they were sometimes called cooperative banks. As Dolores Hayden noted in *Building Suburbia*, the ideas of Thomas Treat Paine, as outlined in his 1881 publication *Own Your Own Home* influenced many people. And so, these building and loan associations were, for a time, very successful, with a reported 1.5 million active members by 1893. The American dream was being developed.

All of this activity set the stage for the urban developments of the twentieth century and the modern cooperative.

# 10
# GOING FORWARD: THE FUTURE OF HOUSING COOPERATIVES

*And where will cooperatives in Washington, D.C., be tomorrow?* The following is a piece from an individual who is very well qualified to discuss cooperatives.

## The Future of Housing Cooperatives in Washington, D.C.

*By Mike O'Dell, director of the DC Cooperative Housing Coalition, and co-owner at Harbour Square since 1985*

As this book has demonstrated, Washington, D.C.'s housing cooperatives have stood the test of time for one hundred years. But what is their future? Since their introduction in the late 1960s, condominiums have become the preferred form of housing of builders and developers in Washington, D.C. The city has 197 recorded housing cooperatives and an unknown but significantly higher number of condominiums. By comparison, New York City's housing cooperatives have been and continue to be the predominant form of personal home ownership, outranking condominiums with a nearly six-to-one ratio. (As of 2012, there were 6,768 co-ops and 1,143 condominiums in New York City.)

So, given the ever-increasing number of condominiums in Washington, D.C., will the city's housing cooperatives survive? The answer to that question is an emphatic, "Yes!"

Existing cooperatives continue to be a preferred form of home ownership for a significant number of buyers, in spite of being the least understood form of residential home ownership. Even with the arrival of condominiums in the 1960s, between 1960 and 2006, forty-five market-rate housing cooperatives have been formed in Washington, including eight new, purposely built cooperatives and thirty-seven conversions from rentals to cooperatives. Collectively, those cooperatives added 5,341 new ownership units to the District's housing inventory.

There are many misunderstandings and myths about the advantages and disadvantages of purchasing a cooperative. For example, unlike New York City cooperatives, with their many hair-raising stories about lengthy and sometimes intrusive board interviews and rejections for odd reasons, the purchasing processes used by Washington, D.C. cooperatives are relatively straightforward. The primary focus is on a buyer's financial ability to purchase into the cooperative.

*What are some of the advantages cooperatives have over condominiums?* In terms of value, cooperative buyers still have an edge over condominium buyers in several financial ways:

- **Cooperatives have lower real estate taxes.** The biggest financial benefit cooperatives have in Washington is a savings in real property taxes. Because the ownership of real property by a cooperative is fundamentally different from the ownership of real property in a condominium, co-op owners usually save on property taxes. A cooperative typically owns a single parcel of property as a whole, but a condominium is divided into multiple separate taxable units. The Cooperative Housing Procedure Act of 1988 provided a uniform procedure and an equitable formula to assess real property owned by cooperatives. This systematic assessment method has resulted in cooperative real property taxes that are typically significantly lower than the aggregate amount of real property taxes on all of the units in a comparable condominium.
- **It is easier to finance major repairs and updates.** To make expensive upgrades or add new amenities, condominiums must either charge owners with special assessments, placing

the onus on owners to determine how they will pay for the assessment, or take on short-term construction loans to pay for major repairs. Condominium associations cannot "mortgage" their buildings. However, cooperatives can obtain long-term financing secured by mortgages on their buildings. Co-ops also have the options of special assessments and short-term financing.

- **Cooperative members may be able to deduct some of the cooperative's expenses on their income taxes.** When a cooperative obtains a "blanket" (also known as an underlying) mortgage for repairs and upgrades, individual members may be eligible for personal income tax deductions for their shares of the cooperative's mortgage interest.
- **Cooperatives have many sources of financing.** Prior to the 1980s, there were few lenders that offered loans for cooperative purchases. That has changed. Most major and local lenders now provide "share loans" for cooperative purchases. These lenders have "recognition agreements" with individual cooperatives that spell out the rights and protections of all parties involved. Terms and rates for these loans are set by the lenders and are usually comparable to condominium unit mortgage loans. Remember, lenders want to lend money and cooperative loans have historically shown extremely low default rates.
- **Cooperatives can command prices competitive with prices for condominium units.** People unfamiliar with cooperatives sometimes assume that cooperative memberships sell for less than comparable condominium units, but comparing apples to apples, that is not necessarily the case. Sales prices for cooperatives, like those for condominiums, are a function of location, amenities, upkeep, management and financial soundness.
- **Cooperative monthly maintenance fees may not be higher—and may even be lower—than condominium fees.** A popular misconception is that cooperative monthly maintenance fees are more expensive than condominium fees. However, on closer inspection, cooperatives may actually be less expensive. Unlike condominium fees, monthly cooperative maintenance fees typically include a portion of the real

property tax (described above) on the cooperative's building and land. In a condominium, each unit owner separately pays their own real property taxes directly to the city. Except for the last purposely built cooperative in 2006, cooperative buildings in Washington are more than fifty years old and, more likely than not, receive single bills for utilities, reflecting bulk purchase discounts in their electric and water utility bills. Newer buildings are often individually metered. Also, monthly fees will vary depending on each building's own amenities, services, staffing and other features. Recognizing all of these factors, there may be little difference between monthly costs in cooperatives and condominiums of similar age, condition, services and amenities.

In addition to financial benefits, there are additional differences that distinguish cooperatives from condominiums. Some of the nonfinancial reasons for opting into cooperative ownership include:

- **Most cooperatives restrict rentals.** Housing cooperatives focus on maximizing the number of resident owners. The primary way to accomplish this is to limit rentals. Depending on the cooperative, rental restrictions in Washington range from not allowing rentals at all to limiting the number of years an owner can rent their unit, with variations on rental restrictions falling in between.
- **Washington cooperatives offer a wealth of architectural gems.** People interested in owning and living in an iconic building with beautiful architecture have many Washington cooperatives to choose from. Cooperatives, as described earlier in this book, offer amazing, grand buildings designed by notable architects, and they are among the *Best Addresses* in Washington. Joining a Washington cooperative is a great way to own a part of and live in a beautiful structure.
- **Cooperatives have a greater sense of community.** Because cooperatives place greater emphasis on maintaining a stable and high-level of owner residency, members are more likely to take a greater interest in their property and their neighbors. As condominiums age and increasingly more units are rented out, the sense of "community" can decline.

Cooperatives and condominiums are also very similar in some ways. They each elect boards of directors, they either hire a management company or are self-managed, they maintain their buildings and grounds and they operate like a small government or business. Cooperatives are not for everyone, but neither are condominiums. Each offers prospective purchasers something unique and desirable. The answer to the question, "Will Washington housing cooperatives survive?" remains an emphatic, "Yes!"

## APPENDIX A

# A LISTING OF WASHINGTON'S MARKET-RATE COOPERATIVES WITH CURRENT AND HISTORICAL DATA

The dates in the tables that follow are generally the completion dates of the listed buildings. In addition, the dates—by year—are when the planned co-op conversions, or planned creations, did actually take place. The construction information has been condensed and was obtained from a number of sources.

# Part One: Locations, sizes and dates

| Name | Address | ZIP | Units | Neighborhood | Year Built | Became a Co-op | City Ward |
|---|---|---|---|---|---|---|---|
| 1300 Mass Owners Co-op, Inc. (The DeSoto) | 1300 Massachusetts Avenue, Northwest | 20005 | 31 | Logan Circle | 1904 | 1976 | 2 |
| 1661 Crescent Place | 1661 Crescent Place, Northwest | 20009 | 55 | Adams Morgan | 1926 | 1926 | 1 |
| 1705 Lanier Cooperative | 1705 Lanier Place, Northwest | 20009 | 30 | Lanier Heights | 1924 | 1924 | 1 |
| 1731 Twentieth Street, Northwest (The Johnson) | 1731 Twentieth Street, Northwest | 20009 | 14 | Dupont Circle | 1901 | 1984 | 1 |
| 1820 Clydesdale Cooperative Inc. | 1820 Clydesdale Place, Northwest | 20009 | 58 | Lanier Heights | 1927 | 1987 | 1 |
| 1832 Biltmore Corporation | 1832 Biltmore Street, Northwest | 20009 | 25 | Adams Morgan | 1907 | 1963 | 1 |
| 1860 California Street Cooperative Inc | 1860 California Street, Northwest | 20009 | 16 | Adams Morgan | 1916 | 1985 | 1 |
| 1860 Clydesdale Place | 1860 Clydesdale Place, Northwest | 20009 | 14 | Lanier Heights | 1927 | 1948 | 1 |
| 1860 Wyoming Avenue | 1860 Wyoming Avenue, Northwest | 20009 | 8 | Adams Morgan | 1952 | 1987 | 1 |
| 1869 Mintwood Place | 1869 Mintwood Place, Northwest | 20009 | 14 | Kalorama Triangle | 1917 | 1981 | 1 |

| Name | Address | ZIP | Units | Neighborhood | Year Built | Became a Co-op | City Ward |
|---|---|---|---|---|---|---|---|
| 1870 Wyoming Avenue, Northwest Inc. | 1870 Wyoming Avenue, Northwest | 20009 | 28 | Kalorama Triangle | 1917 | 1951 | 1 |
| 1901 Wyoming Avenue Cooperative Association (Altamont) | 1901 Wyoming Avenue, Northwest | 20009 | 52 | Kalorama Triangle | 1916 | 1949 | 1 |
| 1915 Sixteenth Street Cooperative | 1915 Sixteenth Street, Northwest | 20009 | 32 | Dupont East | 1923 | 1950 | 1 |
| 2100 Nineteenth Street Cooperative | 2100 Nineteenth Street, Northwest | 20009 | 52 | Adams Morgan | 1928 | 1951 | 1 |
| 2101 Connecticut Avenue Co-op Apartments Inc. | 2101 Connecticut Avenue, Northwest | 20008 | 64 | Kalorama | 1929 | 1976 | 1 |
| 2120 Kalorama Road Co-op | 2120 Kalorama Road, Northwest | 20008 | 4 | Kalorama | 1926 | 1926 | 1 |
| 2301 M Cooperative Association (The Westhaven) | 1200 Twenty-Third Street, Northwest | 20037 | 44 | West End | 1981 | 1981 | 4 |
| 2500 Massachusetts Avenue Co-op | 2500 Massachusetts Avenue, Northwest | 20009 | 8 | Kalorama | 1923 | 1948 | 2 |
| 2520 Forty-First Street, Northwest | 2520 Forty-First Street, Northwest | 20007 | 6 | Glover Park | 1938 | 1980 | 3 |

| Name | Address | ZIP | Units | Neighborhood | Year Built | Became a Co-op | City Ward |
|---|---|---|---|---|---|---|---|
| 2540 Massachusetts Avenue, Northwest Inc. | 2540 Massachusetts Avenue, Northwest | 20008 | 32 | Kalorama Heights | 1926 | 1926 | 2 |
| 2707 Adams Mill Road | 2707 Adams Mill Road, Northwest | 20009 | 50 | Lanier Heights | 1927 | 1927 | 1 |
| 2720 Wisconsin Avenue, Northwest Cooperative | 2720 Wisconsin Avenue, Northwest | 20007 | 49 | Glover Park | 1941 | 1974 | 3 |
| 2852 Ontario Road (The Carrollton) | 2852 Ontario Road, Northwest | 20009 | 6 | Lanier Heights | 1910 | 1910 | 1 |
| 2854 Connecticut Avenue Cooperative | 2854 Connecticut Avenue, Northwest | 20008 | 19 | Woodley Park | 1921 | 1996 | 3 |
| 3001 Porter Street Co-op | 3001 Porter Street, Northwest | 20008 | 13 | Cleveland Park | 1926 | 1926 | 3 |
| 3016 Tilden Sreet, Northwest Inc. | 3016 Tilden Street, Northwest | 20008 | 20 | Cleveland Park | 1928 | 1928 | 3 |
| 3018 Porter Street Northwest Inc. | 3018 Porter Street, Northwest | 20008 | 12 | Cleveland Park | 1925 | 1925 | 3 |
| 3020 Porter Street Northwest Inc. | 3020 Porter Street, Northwest | 20008 | 12 | Cleveland Park | 1925 | 1925 | 3 |
| 3020 Tilden Street Northwest Inc. | 3020 Tilden Street, Northwest | 20008 | 21 | Cleveland Park | 1928 | 1928 | 3 |

| Name | Address | ZIP | Units | Neighborhood | Year Built | Became a Co-op | City Ward |
|---|---|---|---|---|---|---|---|
| 3022 Porter Street Northwest Inc. | 3022 Porter Street, Northwest | 20008 | 12 | Cleveland Park | 1925 | 1925 | 3 |
| 3024 Porter Street Northwest Inc. | 3024 Porter Street, Northwest | 20008 | 12 | Cleveland Park | 1925 | 1925 | 3 |
| 3025 Ontario Road | 3025 Ontario Road, Northwest | 20009 | 45 | Adams Morgan | 1949 | 1986 | 1 |
| 3026 Porter Street Inc. | 3026 Porter Street, Northwest | 20008 | 12 | Cleveland Park | 1925 | 1925 | 3 |
| 3028 Porter Street Inc. | 3028 Porter Street, Northwest | 20008 | 13 | Cleveland Park | 1925 | 1925 | 3 |
| 3407, 3409, 3411 Twenty-Ninth Street, Northwest Inc. | 3407, 3409 and 3411 Twenty-Ninth Street, Northwest | 20008 | 24 | Cleveland Park | 1924 | 1924 | 3 |
| 3620 Connecticut Avenue Cooperative | 3620 Connecticut Avenue, Northwest | 20008 | 19 | Cleveland Park | 1922 | 1947 | 3 |
| 3900 Tunlaw Road, Northwest Cooperative | 3900 Tunlaw Road, Northwest | 20007 | 100 | Glover Park | 1959 | 1979 | 3 |
| 3900 Watson Place Inc. | 3900 Watson Place, Northwest | 20016 | 141 | Cathedral Heights | 1960 | 1963 | 3 |
| 4315 River Road Cooperative Association | 4315 River Road, Northwest | 20016 | 7 | American Univ Park | 1924 | 1951 | 3 |

| Name | Address | ZIP | Units | Neighborhood | Year Built | Became a Co-op | City Ward |
|---|---|---|---|---|---|---|---|
| 5112 Connecticut Avenue Co-op (Connecticut Courts) | 5112 Connecticut Avenue, Northwest | 20008 | 35 | Chevy Chase | 1927 | 1927 | 3 |
| 711–721 Hamlin Street Cooperative | 711–721 Hamlin Street, Northeast | 20017 | 19 | Edgewood | 1937 | 1987 | 5 |
| Arundel Cooperative Inc. | 516 A Street, Northeast | 20002 | 20 | Capitol Hill | 1916 | 1980 | 6 |
| Avondale Cooperative Apartments Inc. | 1734 P Street, Northwest | 20036 | 39 | DuPont Circle | 1914 | 1949 | 2 |
| Beverly Court Cooperative Inc. | 1736 Columbia Road, Northwest | 20009 | 39 | Adams Morgan | 1915 | 1979 | 1 |
| Broadmoor Cooperative Apartments | 3601 Connecticut Avenue, Northwest | 20008 | 194 | Cleveland Park | 1929 | 1948 | 3 |
| Capitol Hill Tower Cooperative | 1000 New Jersey Avenue, Southeast | 20003 | 344 | Capitol Riverfront | 2006 | 2006 | 6 |
| Cathedral Avenue Cooperative | 4101 Cathedral Avenue, Northwest | 20016 | 145 | Cathedral Heights | 1963 | 1978 | 3 |
| Cavanaugh Court Owners Inc. | 1526 Seventeenth Street, Northwest | 20036 | 52 | DuPont Circle | 1917 | 1920 | 2 |
| The Champlain | 2370 Champlain Street, Northwest | 20009 | 13 | Adams Morgan | 1927 | 1984 | 1 |

| Name | Address | ZIP | Units | Neighborhood | Year Built | Became a Co-op | City Ward |
|---|---|---|---|---|---|---|---|
| Chastleton Cooperative | 1701 Sixteenth Street, Northwest | 20009 | 300 | DuPont Circle | 1920 | 2007 | 2 |
| Chesterfield Cooperative | 3315 Wisconsin Avenue, Northwest | 20016 | 66 | Cleveland Park | 1959 | 1978 | 3 |
| Claridge House | 950 Twenty-Fifth Street, Northwest | 20037 | 352 | Foggy Bottom | 1957 | 1979 | 2 |
| Cleveland Cooperative Inc. | 3039 Macomb Street, Northwest | 20008 | 27 | Cleveland Park | 1923 | 1985 | 3 |
| Cleveland Park Cooperative | 3618 Connecticut Avenue, Northwest | 20008 | 18 | Cleveland Park | 1924 | c.1947 | 3 |
| The Clydesdale | 2801 Adams Mill Road, Northwest | 20009 | 52 | Adams Morgan | 1926 | 1926 | 1 |
| Copley Plaza Cooperative | 1514 Seventeenth Street, Northwest | 20036 | 109 | DuPont Circle | 1917 | 1981 | 2 |
| The Devonshire | 2800–2802 Devonshire Place, Northwest | 20008 | 28 | Cleveland Park | 1939 | 1984 | 3 |
| Dumbarton Court | 1657 Thirty-First Street, Northwest | 20007 | 27 | Georgetown | 1910 | 1920 | 2 |
| The Haddington | 1840 Biltmore Street, Northwest | 20009 | 16 | Kalorama Triangle | 1913 | 1987 | 1 |

| Name | Address | ZIP | Units | Neighborhood | Year Built | Became a Co-op | City Ward |
|---|---|---|---|---|---|---|---|
| Harbour Square Owners Inc. | 500 N Street, Southwest | 20024 | 447 | SW Waterfront | 1966 | 1966 | 6 |
| Hawarden Cooperative | 1419 R Street, Northwest | 20009 | 20 | Logan Circle | 1902 | 1949 | 2 |
| Hampshire Gardens | 4912 New Hampshire Avenue, Northwest | 20011 | 102 | Petworth | 1929 | 1929 | 4 |
| Lambert Owners Inc. | 1791 Lanier Place, Northwest | 20009 | 17 | Lanier Heights | 1912 | 1920 | 1 |
| Lehigh Cooperative | 2605 Adams Mill Road, Northwest | 20009 | 12 | Adams Morgan | 1910 | 1947 | 1 |
| Lightview Cooperative | 6606 Georgia Avenue, Northwest | 20012 | 75 | Brightwood | 1955 | 1990 | 4 |
| Madison Terrace Cooperative | 1365 Kennedy Street, Northwest | 20011 | 44 | Brightwood | 1936 | 1983 | 4 |
| The Mendota | 2220 Twentieth Street, Northwest | 20009 | 48 | Kalorama Triangle | 1901 | 1952 | 1 |
| Meridian Hill Studio Cooperative | 2633 Fifteenth Street, Northwest | 20009 | 13 | Columbia Heights | 1923 | 1941 | 1 |
| Mintwood Place Cooperative | 1875 Mintwood Place, Northwest | 20009 | 26 | Kalorama | 1926 | 1990 | 2 |

| Name | Address | ZIP | Units | Neighborhood | Year Built | Became a Co-op | City Ward |
|---|---|---|---|---|---|---|---|
| Naylor Gardens Cooperative | 2725 Thirtieth Street, Southeast | 20020 | 794 | Naylor Gardens | 1943 | 1948 | 7 |
| Netherlands Owners Inc. | 1852 Columbia Road, Northwest | 20009 | 30 | Adams Morgan | 1909 | 1920 | 1 |
| Norfolk Cooperative | 5200–5220 North Capitol Street, Northwest | 20011 | 35 | Fort Totten | 1942 | 1988 | 5 |
| The Northumberland Apartments Inc. | 2039 New Hampshire Avenue Northwest | 20009 | 67 | DuPont Circle | 1910 | 1920 | 2 |
| Ontario Owners Inc. | 2853 Ontario Road, Northwest | 20009 | 120 | Lanier Heights | 1904 | 1953 | 1 |
| Palisades Cooperative | 4581 MacArthur Boulevard, Northwest | 20007 | 11 | Palisades | 1937 | 1990 | 3 |
| Plaza West Cooperative Association Inc. | 1669 Columbia Road, Northwest | 20009 | 53 | Lanier Heights | 1911 | 1989 | 1 |
| Ponce de Leon Cooperative Inc. | 4514 Connecticut Avenue, Northwest | 20008 | 52 | Tenleytown | 1929 | 1972 | 3 |
| Porter Inc. | 3600 Connecticut Avenue, Northwest | 20008 | 28 | Cleveland Park | 1927 | 1927 | 3 |

| Name | Address | ZIP | Units | Neighborhood | Year Built | Became a Co-op | City Ward |
|---|---|---|---|---|---|---|---|
| Potomac Plaza Apartments Cooperative Inc. | 2475 Virginia Avenue, Northwest | 20037 | 273 | Foggy Bottom | 1957 | 1957 | 2 |
| Potomac Plaza Terraces Inc. | 730 Twenty-Fourth Street, Northwest | 20037 | 150 | Foggy Bottom | 1961 | 1961 | 2 |
| The Presidential Cooperative | 1026 Sixteenth Street, Northwest | 20036 | 44 | City Central | 1923 | 1959 | 2 |
| River Park Mutual Homes Inc. | 1301 Delaware Avenue, Southwest | 20024 | 518 | Southwest Waterfront | 1962 | 1962 | 6 |
| Rutland Courts Owners Inc. | 1725 Seventeenth Street, Northwest | 20009 | 79 | DuPont Circle | 1917 | 1920 | 2 |
| The Saxony | 1801 Clydesdale Place, Northwest | 20009 | 161 | Adams Morgan | 1950 | 1984 | 1 |
| Senate Cooperative | 115 Second Street, Northeast | 20002 | 16 | Capitol Hill | 1915 | 1947 | 2 |
| Shoreham West Cooperative Apartments Inc. | 2700 Calvert Street, Northwest | 20008 | 60 | Massachusetts Avenue Heights | 1965 | 1974 | 3 |
| The Stafford | 1789 Lanier Place, Northwest | 20009 | 16 | Adams Morgan | 1911 | 1920 | 1 |

| Name | Address | ZIP | Units | Neighborhood | Year Built | Became a Co-op | City Ward |
|---|---|---|---|---|---|---|---|
| Tiber Island Cooperative Homes Inc. | 429 N Street, Southwest | 20024 | 389 | Southwest Waterfront | 1965 | 1982 | 6 |
| Tilden Gardens Inc. | 3000 Tilden Street, Northwest | 20008 | 170 | North Cleveland Park | 1930 | 1939 | 3 |
| Van Ness North Cooperative Inc. | 3001 Veazey Terrace, Northwest | 20008 | 461 | Forest Hills | 1967 | 1979 | 3 |
| Watergate East Inc. | 2510 Virginia Avenue, Northwest | 20037 | 240 | Foggy Bottom | 1965 | 1965 | 2 |
| Watergate South Inc. | 700 New Hampshire Avenue, Northwest | 20037 | 230 | Foggy Bottom | 1970 | 1970 | 2 |
| Watergate West Inc. | 2700 Virginia Avenue, Northwest | 20037 | 143 | Foggy Bottom | 1968 | 1968 | 2 |
| Westchester Corporation | 4000 Cathedral Avenue, Northwest | 20016 | 520 | Cathedral Heights | 1931 | 1953 | 2 |
| Westmoreland Cooperative | 2122 California Street, Northwest | 20008 | 60 | Kalorama | 1906 | 1948 | 2 |
| Winchester Underwood Cooperative | 6445 Luzon Avenue, Northwest | 20012 | 81 | Brightwood | 1960 | 2000 | 4 |
| The Woodrow | 1835 Phelps Place, Northwest | 20008 | 25 | Kalorama | 1925 | 1949 | 2 |

# Part Two: Architects, Developers and Builders

| Name | Address | Architect | Developer | Builder |
|---|---|---|---|---|
| 1300 Mass Owners Co-op Inc. (The DeSoto) | 1300 Massachusetts Avenue, Northwest | Hunter & Bell | Bates Warren | Bates Warren |
| 1661 Crescent Place | 1661 Crescent Place, Northwest | Joseph Younger | Monroe and R. Bates Warren | M. and R.B. Warren |
| 1705 Lanier Cooperative | 1705 Lanier Place, Northwest | James E. Cooper | Monroe and R. Bates Warren | M. and R.B. Warren |
| 1731 Twentieth Street, Northwest (The Johnson) | 1731 Twentieth Street, Northwest | Speiden & Speiden | Annie S. Terrell and Hester V. Johnson | J.H. Hudson |
| 1820 Clydesdale Cooperative Inc. | 1820 Clydesdale Place, Northwest | George T. Santmyers | Charles D. Sager | Charles D. Sager |
| 1832 Biltmore Corporation | 1832 Biltmore Street, Northwest | Nicholas R. Grimm | Harry Wardman | Wardman Construction Co. |
| 1860 California Street Cooperative Inc. | 1860 California Street, Northwest | Albert M. Schneider | Harry Wardman | Wardman Construction Co. |
| 1860 Clydesdale Place | 1860 Clydesdale Place, Northwest | Harvey H. Warwick Sr. | Morris Cafritz | Cafritz Construction Co. |
| 1860 Wyoming Avenue | 1860 Wyoming Avenue, Northwest | | Adams Investment Corporation | Adams Investment Corp. |
| 1869 Mintwood Place | 1869 Mintwood Place, Northwest | Merrill Vaughan | Berkeley L. Simmons | Edward McGee |

| Name | Address | Architect | Developer | Builder |
|---|---|---|---|---|
| 1870 Wyoming Avenue, Northwest Inc. | 1870 Wyoming Avenue, Northwest | B. Stanley Simmons | John L. Barr | John L. Barr |
| 1901 Wyoming Avenue Cooperative Association (Altamont) | 1901 Wyoming Avenue, Northwest | Arthur B. Heaton | George Truesdell | Davis Construction Co. |
| 1915 Sixteenth Street Cooperative | 1915 Sixteenth Street, Northwest | David L. Stern and Stern & Tomlinson | A. Liebman & S. Kaufman | Stern & Tomlinson |
| 2100 Nineteenth Street Cooperative | 2100 Nineteenth Street, Northwest | Joseph W. Geddes | Rose G. Casey | I.B. Thonias |
| 2101 Connecticut Ave. Co-op Apartments Inc. | 2101 Connecticut Avenue, Northwest | George T. Santmyers and Joseph Abel | Harry M. Bralove (2101 Conn Avenue Inc.) | Harry M. Bralove |
| 2120 Kalorama Road Co-op | 2120 Kalorama Road, Northwest | Louis Justement | Clifford Bangs | Clifford Bangs |
| 2301 M Cooperative Association (The Westhaven) | 1200 Twenty-Third Street, Northwest | | M & 23 Partnership | |
| 2500 Massachusetts Avenue Co-op | 2500 Massachusetts Avenue, Northwest | Sholtes & Co. | W.H. Gottlieb & L.E. Sholtes | Sholtes & Co. |

| Name | Address | Architect | Developer | Builder |
|---|---|---|---|---|
| 2520 Forty-First Street, Northwest | 2520 Forty-First Street, Northwest | George T. Santmyers | Maurice Korman | Maurice Korman |
| 2540 Massachusetts Avenue, Northwest Inc. | 2540 Massachusetts Avenue, Northwest | Harry L. Edwards | Monroe and R. Bates Warren | M. and R.B. Warren |
| 2707 Adams Mill Road | 2707 Adams Mill Road, Northwest | George T. Santmyers | Charles Hunt | Charles Hunt |
| 2720 Wisconsin Avenue, Northwest Cooperative | 2720 Wisconsin Avenue, Northwest | Joseph H. Abel and Dillon & Abel | Henry K. Jawish | Henry K. Jawish |
| 2852 Ontario Road (The Carrollton) | 2852 Ontario Road, Northwest | Appleton P. Clark Jr. | Carrollton Apartment House Co. | Gormley-Poynton Co. |
| 2854 Connecticut Avenue Cooperative | 2854 Connecticut Avenue, Northwest | Eugene Waggaman | Harry Wardman | Wardman Construction Co. |
| 3001 Porter Street Co-op | 3001 Porter Street, Northwest | James E. Cooper | Monroe and R. Bates Warren | M. and R.B. Warren |
| 3016 Tilden Sreet, Northwest Inc. | 3016 Tilden Street, Northwest | Harry L. Edwards, with Parks & Baxter | Monroe and R. Bates Warren | M. and R.B. Warren |
| 3018 Porter Street Northwest Inc. | 3018 Porter Street, Northwest | James E. Cooper | Monroe and R. Bates Warren | M. and R.B. Warren |

| Name | Address | Architect | Developer | Builder |
|---|---|---|---|---|
| 3020 Porter Street Northwest Inc. | 3020 Porter Street, Northwest | James E. Cooper | Monroe and R. Bates Warren | M. and R.B. Warren |
| 3020 Tilden Street Northwest Inc. | 3020 Tilden Street, Northwest | Harry L. Edwards, with Parks & Baxter | Monroe and R. Bates Warren | M. and R.B. Warren |
| 3022 Porter Street Northwest Inc. | 3022 Porter Street, Northwest | James E. Cooper | Monroe and R. Bates Warren | M. and R.B. Warren |
| 3024 Porter Street Northwest Inc. | 3024 Porter Street, Northwest | James E. Cooper | Monroe and R. Bates Warren | M. and R.B. Warren |
| 3025 Ontario Road | 3025 Ontario Road, Northwest | Leon Brown | Meyer Seigel | Lenkin Construction Co. |
| 3026 Porter Street Inc. | 3026 Porter Street, Northwest | James E. Cooper | Monroe and R. Bates Warren | M. and R.B. Warren |
| 3028 Porter Street Inc. | 3028 Porter Street, Northwest | James E. Cooper | Monroe and R. Bates Warren | M. and R.B. Warren |
| 3407, 3409 and 3411 Twenty-Ninth Street, Northwest Inc. | 3407, 3409 and 3411 Twenty-Ninth Street, Northwest | G. Neal Bell | Monroe and R. Bates Warren | M. and R.B. Warren |
| 3620 Connecticut Avenue Cooperative | 3620 Connecticut Avenue, Northwest | Stern & Tomlinson | L.G. White | L.G. White |

| Name | Address | Architect | Developer | Builder |
|---|---|---|---|---|
| 3900 Tunlaw Road, Northwest Cooperative | 3900 Tunlaw Road, Northwest | | Clement C. Alpert | Clement C. Alpert |
| 3900 Watson Place Inc. | 3900 Watson Place, Northwest | Harry Price and Berla & Abel | Real Estate Corp. | Real Estate Corp. |
| 4315 River Road Cooperative Association | 4315 River Road, Northwest | E.C. Kinnear | G.K. Gish | G.K. Gish |
| 5112 Connecticut Avenue Co-op (Connecticut Courts) | 5112 Connecticut Avenue, Northwest | Doleman & McCaw | Harry A. Brannow | Harry A. Brannow |
| 711–721 Hamlin Street Cooperative | 711–721 Hamlin Street, Northeast | George T. Santmyers | Dallas M. Grady | Dallas M. Grady |
| Arundel Cooperative Inc. | 516 A Street, Northeast | Thomas W. Smith | Thomas W. Smith | J.L. Parsons |
| Avondale Cooperative Apartments Inc. | 1734 P Street, Northwest | Frank Russell White | Harry Wardman | Wardman Construction Co. |
| Beverly Court Cooperative Inc. | 1736 Columbia Road, Northwest | Hunter & Bell | William L. Browning for Bates Warren | Fox & Lewis |
| Broadmoor Cooperative Apartments | 3601 Connecticut Avenue, Northwest | Joseph H. Abel | Harry M. Bralove and Edward C. Ernst | Harry M. Bralove |

| Name | Address | Architect | Developer | Builder |
|---|---|---|---|---|
| Capitol Hill Tower Cooperative | 1000 New Jersey Avenue, Southeast | | NJA Development Partners | NJA Develop. Partners |
| Cathedral Avenue Cooperative | 4101 Cathedral Avenue, Northwest | Corning, Elmore and Fischer | Stuart A. Bernstein and John J. Mason | |
| Cavanaugh Court Owners Inc. | 1526 Seventeenth Street, Northwest | Albert M. Schneider | Harry Wardman | Wardman Construction Co. |
| The Champlain | 2370 Champlain Street, Northwest | Claughton West | G.G. Loehler | G.G. Loehler Co. |
| Chastleton Cooperative | 1701 Sixteenth Street, Northwest | Philip M. Jullien | S.W. Strauss Co. and District Apartment Co | Wire Granit Construction Co. |
| Chesterfield Cooperative | 3315 Wisconsin Avenue, Northwest | Robert Lowe | Robert Lowe | Robert Lowe |
| Claridge House (Investors allowed) | 950 Twenty-Fifth Street, Northwest | | The Potomac House Inc. | |
| Cleveland Cooperative Inc. | 3039 Macomb Street, Northwest | Milburn-Heister & Co. | Parsons & Hyman Inc. | Parsons & Hyman, Inc. |
| Cleveland Park Cooperative | 3618 Connecticut Avenue, Northwest | Stern & Tomlinson | L.G. White | L.G. White |
| The Clydesdale | 2801 Adams Mill Road, Northwest | Wardman Construction Co. | Harry Wardman | Wardman Construction Co. |

| Name | Address | Architect | Developer | Builder |
|---|---|---|---|---|
| Copley Plaza Cooperative | 1514 Seventeenth Street, Northwest | Albert M. Schneider | Harry Wardman | Wardman Construction Co. |
| The Devonshire | 2800–2802 Devonshire Place, Northwest | George T. Santmyers | Cortland Construction Co. | Cortland Construction Co. |
| Dumbarton Court | 1657 Thirty-First Street, Northwest | George S. Cooper | George S. Cooper | George S. Cooper |
| The Haddington | 1840 Biltmore Street, Northwest | George N. Ray | Berkeley L. Simmons | Edward McGee |
| Harbour Square Owners Inc. | 500 N Street, Southwest | Chloethiel Woodard Smith, with Daniel Urban Kiley | Shannon & Luchs | John McShain Construction |
| Hawarden Cooperative | 1419 R Street, Northwest | George S. Cooper | Gladstone Apartment House Co. | John H. Nolan |
| Hampshire Gardens | 4912 New Hampshire Avenue, Northwest | George T. Santmyers and James E. Cooper | Hampshire Gardens Development Corp. | Shapiro Construction Co. |
| Lambert Owners Inc. | 1791 Lanier Place, Northwest | Hunter & Bell | William Sholes for Bates Warren | Fox & Lewis |
| Lehigh Cooperative | 2605 Adams Mill Road, Northwest | Hunter & Bell | John L. Warren | John L. Warren |

| Name | Address | Architect | Developer | Builder |
| --- | --- | --- | --- | --- |
| Lightview Cooperative | 6606 Georgia Avenue, Northwest | Lightview Development Co. | Lightview Development Co. | Lightview Development Co. |
| Madison Terrace Cooperative | 1365 Kennedy Street, Northwest | Harvey P. Baxter | Madison Terrace Corp. | Madison Terrace Corp. |
| The Mendota | 2220 Twentieth Street, Northwest | James G. Hill | Iowa Apartment House Co. | J.L. Marshall |
| Meridian Hill Studio Cooperative | 2633 Fifteenth Street, Northwest | George Oakley Totten Jr. | Meridian Hill Club (Mary Henderson) | Snowden Ashford |
| Mintwood Place Cooperative | 1875 Mintwood Place, Northwest | George T. Santmyers | Harry M. Bralove | Harry M. Bralove |
| Naylor Gardens Cooperative | 2725 Thirtieth Street, Southeast | Kenneth Franzheim | Defense Homes Corp. | Chas. H. Tompkins Co. |
| Netherlands Owners Inc. | 1852 Columbia Road, Northwest | Hunter & Bell | Bates Warren | Bates Warren |
| Norfolk Cooperative | 5200, 5210 and 5220 North Capitol Street, Northwest | George T. Santmyers | D.J. Dunigan, Inc. | D.J. Dunigan |
| The Northumberland Apartments Inc. | 2039 New Hampshire Avenue, Northwest | Albert M. Beers | Harry Wardman | Wardman Construction Co. |
| Ontario Owners Inc. | 2853 Ontario Road, Northwest | Hill and Kendall | Ontario Apartment House Co. | J.L. Marshall |

| Name | Address | Architect | Developer | Builder |
|---|---|---|---|---|
| Palisades Cooperative | 4581 MacArthur Boulevard, Northwest | William Crusemire | William Crusemire | William Crusemire |
| Plaza West Cooperative Association Inc. | 1669 Columbia Road, Northwest | B. Stanley Simmons | Louis A. Pirie | Gormley-Poynton Co. |
| Ponce de Leon Cooperative Inc. | 4514 Connecticut Avenue, Northwest | David L. Stern and Stern & Tomlinson | David L. Stern | Stern & Tomlinson |
| Porter Inc. | 3600 Connecticut Avenue, Northwest | Harvey H. Warwick Sr. | Morris Cafritz | Cafritz Construction Co. |
| Potomac Plaza Apartments Cooperative Inc. | 2475 Virginia Avenue, Northwest | Dixon & Weppner | George P. Marshall et al., Edmund J. Flynn | Hageman-Harris Co. |
| Potomac Plaza Terraces Inc. | 730 Twenty-Fourth Street, Northwest | F. Wallace Dixon & Associates | Euram Corporation and Edmund J. Flynn | Magazine Bros. Construction |
| The Presidential Cooperative | 1026 Sixteenth Street, Northwest | Appleton P. Clark Jr. | Clara R. Dennis | Parsons & Hyman Inc. |
| River Park Mutual Homes Inc. | 1301 Delaware Avenue, Southwest | Charles M. Goodman | Reynolds Metals Development Corp | Reynolds Metals Dev. Corp |
| Rutland Courts Owners Inc. | 1725 Seventeenth Street, Northwest | Wardman Construction Co. | Harry Wardman | Wardman Construction Co. |

| Name | Address | Architect | Developer | Builder |
|---|---|---|---|---|
| The Saxony | 1801 Clydesdale Place, Northwest | Milton J. Prassas | Adams Mill Plaza Inc. | Charles E. Smith & Co. |
| Senate Cooperative | 115 Second Street, Northwest | George P. Stales | S.A. Manuel | Peter Fersinger |
| Shoreham West Cooperative Apartments Inc. | 2700 Calvert Street, Northwest | Emery Roth & Sons, with Vlastimil Koubek | Harry M. Bralove | Harry M. Bralove |
| The Stafford | 1789 Lanier Place, Northwest | Hunter & Bell | William H. Sholes for Bates Warren | W.H. Sholes |
| Tiber Island Cooperative Homes Inc. | 429 N Street, Southwest | Keyes, Lethbridge and Condon | Berens Company | Charles H. Tompkins Co. |
| Tilden Gardens Inc. | 3000 Tilden Street, Northwest | Harry L. Edwards, with Parks & Baxter | Monroe and R. Bates Warren | M. and R.B. Warren |
| Van Ness North Cooperative Inc. | 3001 Veazey Terrace, Northwest | Abel & Weinstein | Robert I. Silverman | Southeast Construction Co. |
| Watergate East Inc. | 2510 Virginia Avenue, Northwest | Luigi Moretti, with Fischer and Elmore | Societa Generale Immobiliare | Magazine Bros. Construction |
| Watergate South Inc. | 700 New Hampshire Avenue, Northwest | Luigi Moretti, with Fischer and Elmore | Societa Generale Immobiliare | Magazine Bros. Construction |

| Name | Address | Architect | Developer | Builder |
| --- | --- | --- | --- | --- |
| Watergate West Inc. | 2700 Virginia Avenue, Northwest | Luigi Moretti, with Fischer and Elmore | Societa Generale Immobiliare | Magazine Bros. Construction |
| Westchester Corporation | 4000 Cathedral Avenue, Northwest | Harvey H. Warwick Sr. | Gustave Ring and Westchester Corp. | Westchester Dev. Corp. |
| Westmoreland Cooperative | 2122 California Street, Northwest | Edgar S. Kennedy & Harry Blake | Kennedy & Davis Co. | Kennedy & Davis Co. |
| Winchester Underwood Cooperative | 6445 Luzon Avenue, Northwest | | Joseph B. Shapiro | Shapiro Construction Co. |
| The Woodrow | 1835 Phelps Place, Northwest | David L. Stern and Stern & Tomlinson | W.T. Powell | W.T. Powell |

## APPENDIX B

# THE YEAR 2020: IMAGES OF THE MEMBER CO-OPS OF THE DC COOPERATIVE HOUSING COALITION

The following set of photographs are contemporary images of the member cooperatives of the DC Cooperative Housing Coalition. They nicely display the wonderful variety of housing associations in the city.

*Unless otherwise noted, the following photographs are courtesy of the DC Cooperative Housing Coalition.*

The Westchester Cooperative, 4000 Cathedral Avenue, Northwest.

*Clockwise from top left*: The 1915 Sixteenth Street Cooperative, Northwest; 1870 Wyoming Avenue, Northwest, in Kalorama Triangle; 1705 Lanier Place, Northwest, in Lanier Heights; 2101 Connecticu Avenue, Northwest, in Kalorama; 2120 Kalorama Road, Northwest; The Altamont, 1901 Wyoming Avenue, Northwest.

The Palisades Cooperative, 4851 MacArthur Boulevard, Northwest. *Photograph by the author.*

The Broadmoor Cooperative, 3900 Connecticut Avenue, Northwest.

Beverly Court, 1736 Columbia Road, Northwest.

*Clockwise from top left*: 1832 Biltmore Street, Northwest. *Photograph by the author*; 2720 Wisconsin Avenue, Northwest; The Lambert Co-op, 1791 Lanier Place, Northwest; Shoreham West Cooperative, 2700 Calvert Street, Northwest.

*ckwise from top left*: Hawarden Cooperative, 1419 R Street, Northwest; The Porter, 3600 Connecticut enue, Northwest; 3020 Tilden Street, Northwest, in Cleveland Park; Avondale Cooperative artments, 1734 P Street, Northwest.

*Clockwise from top left*: Cavanaugh Court, 2222 Seventeenth Street, Northwest; 2854 Connecticut Avenue, Northwest, in Cleveland Park; Cathedral Avenue Co-op, 4101 Cathedral Avenue, Northwest; The Cleveland Cooperative, 3039 Macomb Street, Northwest; 3026 Porter Street, in Cleveland Park; 3407–3411 Twenty-Ninth Street, Northwest, in Cleveland Park.

*ckwise from top left*: Chastleton Cooperative, 1701 Sixteenth Street, Northwest; 3016 Tilden Street, rthwest, in Cleveland Park; Mintwood Place Co-op, 1875 Mintwood Place, Northwest; The Ontario, 53 Ontario Road, Northwest, in Lanier Heights; Lehigh Cooperative, 2605 Adams Mill Road, rthwest; The Haddington, 1840 Biltmore Street, Northwest. *Photographs by the author.*

*Clockwise from top left*: 3620 Connecticut Avenue, Northwest; Westmoreland Cooperative, 2122 Californ Street, Northwest; Rutland Courts, 1725 Seventeenth Street, Northwest, in Dupont Circle; Plaza West Cooperative, 1669 Columbia Road, Northwest.

Tiber Island Cooperative, 429 N Street, Southwest.

Harbour Square Cooperative, 500 N Street, Southwest.

Watergate East Cooperative, 2510 Virginia Avenue, Northwest.

*Clockwise from top left*: Naylor Gardens Cooperative, 2725 Thirtieth Street, Southeast; 1661 Crescent Place, Northwest, in Meridian Hill; Ponce de Leon Cooperative, 4514 Connecticut Avenue, Northwes Netherlands Cooperative, 1852 Columbia Road, Northwest; 2100 Nineteenth Street Cooperative, Northwest, in Adams Morgan; Potomac Plaza Cooperative, 2475 Virginia Avenue, Northwest.

*ckwise from top left*: Watergate South operative, 700 New Hampshire Avenue, rthwest; Hampshire Gardens, 250 Farragut eet, Northwest. *Photograph by the author;* 5 River Road, upper Northwest; 5112 nnecticut Avenue, Northwest.

*Clockwise from top left*: Copley Plaza Cooperative, 1514 Seventeenth Street, Northwest; The 711–721 Hamlin Street Cooperative, Northeast; Capitol Hill Tower Co-op, 1000 New Jersey Avenue, Southeas The Presidential Cooperative, 1026 Sixteenth Street, Northwest; The DeSoto, 1300 Massachusetts Avenue, Northwest; 1869 Mintwood Place, Northwest.

3024 Porter Street, Northwest, in Cleveland Park. *Photograph by the author.*

River Park Mutual Homes, 1301 Delaware Avenue, Southwest.

2500 Massachusetts Avenue, Northwest.

*Clockwise from top left*: 2540 Massachusetts Avenue, Northwest; 3900 Watson Place, Northwest, in Cathedral Heights; Madison Terrace Co-op, 1365 Kennedy Street, Northwest; Van Ness North Cooperative, 3001 Veazey Terrace, Northwest; 1820 Clydesdale Place, Northwest, in Lanier Heights; 2707 Adams Mill Road, Northwest, in Lanier Heights.

*Top*: Winchester Underwood Co-op, 6445 Luzon Avenue, Northwest.
*Middle*: Norfolk Cooperative, 5200 North Capitol Street, Northwest.
*Bottom*: Lightview Cooperative, 6606 Georgia Avenue, Northwest.

*Clockwise from top left*: The Saxony, 1801 Clydesdale Place, Northwest. *Photograph by the author*; Tilden Gardens, 3000 Connective Avenue, Northwest; Th Arundel, 516 A Street, Northeast. *Photograph by the author*; 1860 Wyoming Avenue, Northwest. *Photograp by the author*; Chesterfield Cooperative, 3315 Wisconsin Avenue, Northwest.

# BIBLIOGRAPHY


DeFerrari, John. *Lost Washington, D.C.* Charleston, SC: The History Press, 2011.

Goode, James M. *Best Addresses: A Century of Washington's Distinguished Apartment Houses*. Washington, D.C.: Smithsonian Institution Press, 2003.

Green, Constance McLaughlin. *Washington: A History of the Capital, 1800-1950*. Princeton, NJ: Princeton University Press, 1977.

Hands, John. *Housing Co-operatives*. Washington, D.C.: Society for Co-operative Dwellings, 1975.

Hansen, Stephen A. *Kalorama Triangle: The History of a Capital Neighborhood*. Charleston, SC: The History Press, 2011.

Karas, William M. *Co-operatively Speaking*. Washington, D.C.: Edmund J. Flynn Company, 2000.

Leabman, Arthur, ed. *Co-ops 101*. Washington, D.C.: DC Cooperative Housing Coalition, 2012.

Longstreth, Richard. *Housing Washington, Two Centuries of Residential Development*. Chicago: Center for American Places at Columbia College-Chicago, 2010.

McKevitt, Stephen. *Meridian Hill: A History*. Charleston, SC: The History Press, 2014.

Moeller, G. Martin, Jr. *AIA Guide to the Architecture of Washington, D.C.* Baltimore, MD: Johns Hopkins University Press, 2012.

Protopappas, John J., and Judith Meany. *Washington on Foot*. Washington, D.C.: Smithsonian Books, 2012.

Slauson, Alan B. *A History of the City of Washington, Its Men and Institutions*. Washington, D.C.: *Washington Post* Co., 1903.

Smith, Kathryn S. *Washington at Home: An Illustrated History of Neighborhoods in the Nation's Capital*. Baltimore, MD: Johns Hopkins University Press, 1988.

Williams, Paul K., and Gregory J. Alexander. *Woodley Park*. Charleston, SC: Arcadia Press, 2003.

## *Additional Sources*

Cooperative Websites
- Broadmoor
- Harbour Square
- Ontario
- Presidential
- River Park
- Tilden Gardens
- Van Ness North
- Westchester

District of Columbia Government
- D.C. Public Library, Washingtoniana Collection
- Office of Planning and Historic Preservation Office
- Office of the Surveyor (Department of Consumer and Regulatory Affairs)
- Recorder of Deeds

George Washington University

Google

Historical Society of Washington, D.C.
Library of Congress
National Archives
U.S. Commission of Fine Arts
*Washington Evening Star*
*Washington Post*
Wikidata

# INDEX

## Numerals

## A



## B



## C



## D

## J



## K



## L



## M



## N



## O

## P



## R



## S



## T

## V



## W



## Y

# ABOUT THE AUTHOR

Today, Steve McKevitt lives in a mid-size co-op in Adams Morgan in Washington, D.C. He was born in Washington, D.C., and grew up locally in Silver Spring. Steve is proud to be a native Washingtonian. After living in Wisconsin for a time, he returned to the District and, for many years, worked for the federal government. Now that he is retired, he has recently been occupied with exploring the many aspects of Washington's civic and cultural history. He is a board member of the DC Cooperative Housing Coalition and is also a member of the Historical Society of Washington, D.C. In addition, he is a member of several local neighborhood groups. Steve is a strong believer in the concept of housing cooperatives; he considers them to be good for a city's environment and good homes for city residents.